Faith Fuel for Journey written by Clifford F. Wright is filled with real stories about real people, including the author about how God provided them with *faith fuel* just when they were about to run out. He will do the same for you.

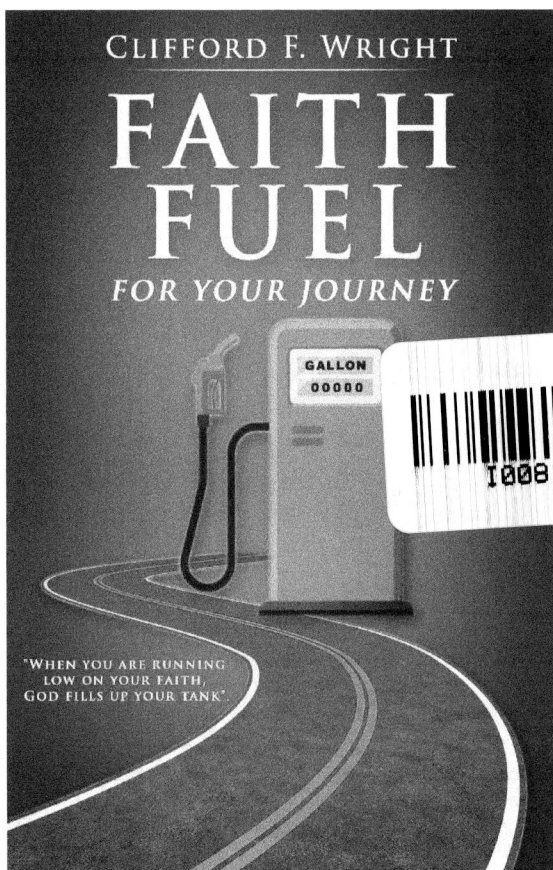

CLIFFORD F. WRIGHT

FAITH FUEL

FOR YOUR JOURNEY

GALLON
00000

"WHEN YOU ARE RUNNING
LOW ON YOUR FAITH,
GOD FILLS UP YOUR TANK".

ENDORSEMENTS

Life takes us to places where it is difficult to continue moving forward. However, when we keep moving toward our dreams, we are fueled and inspired to continue on our journey and go beyond our human ability. It's called faith.

Cliff's approach and writing style Keeps your attention while you read powerful stories by everyday people who overcame life pitfalls and setbacks.

I highly recommend "Faith Fuel for Your Journey". It will capture your attention early, giving you inspiration and a clear pathway forward.

Faith, is often misunderstood because we believe our achievements are a result of our own faith. No, It's less about our own faith but Who we place our faith in. Placing our faith and trust in God, the creator of heaven and earth, we will discover how a life of faith will bring us a more fulfilling life.
Faith will Find a Way!

Bishop Ed Smith
Zoe Association International Founder
Nehemiah ProjectLA

Clifford Wright takes us on an inspiring, authentic, challenging, and hands-on ride in the pages of *'Faith Fuel for Your Journey'*. Blending powerful scriptural insight with relevant and genuine stories from his own life, Cliff offers us a way to both understand and live out the *'faith journey'* for which each of us is designed. Every chapter provides clarity around different elements of faith and encourages us to live it now, knowing we never need run out of 'faith fuel', even in the midst of a desert.

Timely insight for all of us and needed now more than ever, *'Faith Fuel for Your Journey'* provides hope and inspiration today!

Having the privilege of training Clifford Wright as an Awyken Life Purpose Coach and further as an Awyken Coach Trainer, I know he lives daily the principles presented in his book. Observing him over the past year and a half as he has stepped more fully and completely by faith into his purpose, and seeing the resulting favor that has accompanied his obedience, Cliff has inspired and challenged me to do the same. He is a great author, coach, trainer, and most importantly, friend! I look forward to all that God has in store for him, for I know it is amazing!

David Kobelin

Awyken Master Trainer

Identity Restoration Specialist at ClarityCoach

Younique Master Trainer

SPECIAL DEDICATION

Just before the publishing of my second book, "**Faith Fuel for Your Journey**", my first cousin, Gary Davis completed his life's journey on April 14. 2022. He lived life full of love, humor and laughter. Gary did not sit on his gifts. He traveled the world, and performed in Asia as a singer and musician. Gary was also a talented songwriter. His exciting journey included recording two singles, "Boat of Love" and "God Bless Our Love", inspired by his romantic marriage to Rebecca McMullin-Davis. Gary loved his daughters, April Tabor, Sheret Donyal, Angelle Davis, Taa Davis, and his grandchildren. He always showed love for his sisters, Glenda McGilvery, Barbara Davis–Bass and Catherine Berry, a host of nieces, nephews, cousins and his aunt, Freddie Mae Branch. I am praying for the Lord to fill all of us up with *Faith Fuel* for the rest of our journey together without Gary being in the driver's seat.

DEDICATION

 "*Faith for Your Journey*" is dedicated to the One who foreknew and planned my life's journey, my Father God, through Jesus Christ my Lord and Savior. I also honor the memory of my parents and my wife's parents. My father Roger Hugh Wright, mother, Willie Nell Wright and parents-in-love, James Talley King and Mattiie King are all watching over us on our journey from Heaven.

SPECIAL THANKS

My wife of more than 39 years and girlfriend for two years, Sondria, is truly the woman that God sent me. He made sure we met at the most critical time of my life. She is truly the G.L.U. (God's Love Unveiled) that has held our family together! Had it not been for meeting this beautiful woman, my journey would have more than likely been a wreck. I thank you babe for being here with me through thick and thin, ups and downs. I am so thankful that you continue to stand by me. It is because of you, our children, and grandchildren that I have the WHY to continue on my journey. Thank you for being my unpaid and unofficial proofreader. You helped me tremendously with writing the book. I love you and appreciate you more today than ever.

To my oldest son, Cliff II, I love you son! You have been my strongest motivator who has helped me grow as a father. I thank you for your love, patience and compassion. I am so proud of you. You are a faithful father to Savion and Zaire and loving husband to Blanca. You are a tremendous example of how to continue on your life's journey even when the road gets rough. I love you.

Driana (Dri Dri), I could not have prayed for a better daughter! You have always honored your Mom and me. I know that God is pleased with you. I am so blessed that I got to walk you down the aisle when you and Richard got married. Your commitment to be a virgin until you got married was a dream come true for both your Mom and I. I am proud of you and Richard. You are both wonderful parents to our granddaughters, Chelsea and Madison. You know I love them so much!

Richard, I want you to know that when you asked Sondria and I for our blessing to ask Driana to marry you, giving our blessings was the best decision we could have made. You are such a caring dad to Chelsea and Madison and loving husband to Driana. Although I never saw it coming, your decision to move your family to New York was the best choice for you all. Sondria and I are proud of how you provide for your family and excel in your career.

To my youngest son, Jy, I cannot say it enough how proud your Mom and I are of you for being the loving and faithful Dad to Michael. You are such a loving son. I enjoy our many conversations about God, life and living a life of purpose. You are truly a trailblazer! I have no doubts that you will accomplish all of your dreams and goals. I love you son!

To my grandchildren, Savion, Zaire, Michael, Chelsea and Madison, I thank God for you. I know that He has a plan for your life that will be good. He will cause you to experience the best that life has to offer. My prayer is that you will always have "**Faith Fuel for Your Journey**". Papa is proud of you and loves you!

To our aunts, uncles, cousins, nieces and nephews, I thank God for you and love you all!

There are too many people I need to thank to place in this book. So if you don't see your name, it is not because I don't appreciate and love you. I would have to write a whole book to list everyone's name. There are however some of my family, loved-ones, mentors and friends I must acknowledge.

Minister Patricia Wyatt, Not Forgotten Ministries, you know Sondria and I love you Sis! You and I have ministered together for almost 30 years. You have been in the trenches with me and seen my ups and downs more than anyone except my wife. I thank God that He has placed you on my journey!

To Apostle Cassanolia Williams and Pastor Brenda Williams of Victory Outreach International Seed Ministry, I don't have enough words to adequately express how much I love you and how much of a blessing you all have been to me and my family. Thank you for believing in what God has put inside of me and loving me like your own son and brother!

To Bishop Ed Smith and First Lady, Vanessa, pastors Emeritus of Zoe Christian Fellowship of Whittier, Founders of Nehemiah L.A. and Awyken Life Purpose Coaching Ministry, the two of you have been a shining example of how to be faithful to my God-given assignment. Watching you for more than 30 years of serving God's people and knowing you for more than 46 years has added *Faith Fuel for My Journey*.

To Coach David Kobelin, Master Trainer of Awyken Life Purpose Coaching Ministry, I am so thankful to the Lord for ordering my steps that led me to be coached by you. God used you in so many ways, including coaching that produced clarity and accountability in my mind. Becoming a Certified, Awyken Coach and future Trainer, has helped me to identify my vision, and develop an action plan. My book, *Faith Fuel for Your Journey* is just one of the many things I have accomplished since receiving your coaching. God bless you and your wife, Julianne.

To Pastors Keithalan and Maral Hinson, Purpose Place Church L.A. Sondria, Jy and I thank God for you and your family. Through you and your ministry gifts, God has demonstrated His love, signs and wonders in our lives. We love you, your family and the Purpose Place L.A. family!

I want to thank Ms. Guernica Williams, After 6 Media for her excellent work in editing my book. She is very professional and reliable. If you need an editor for the books you write, I highly recommend her. You reach Ms. Williams at www.after6mediallc.com

SPECIAL ACKNOWLEDGMENTS

In addition to the special thanks, I need to acknowledge the following giving individuals who God has used to add *fuel* to my *faith* tank and be a blessing to me on my journey. Each one of them was very vital in *Faith Fuel for Your Journey* being published.

Dr. Shari D. Scott, Founder of Developing Healthy Desires Ministries and Author of *Wisdom to Serve: Servant Leadership in a Volatile World* and *Wounded Hearts Made Whole*.

Evangelist Vickie Harris Trigg who is so thoughtful and goes out her way to be a blessing to others and support their vision. Her motto is "She is Saved to Serve", which fits her perfectly.

Pastor Chandra Robinson, One Nation Under God Christian Church and CEO of Hope Alive Counseling Centers who has been faithfully serving God's forgotten people for more than 25 years along with her mother, Pastor Ceola Robinson

Marie Zoutomou-Quintanilla, host and executive producer of National TV Show and Book "Don't Worry, You Are Being Tested." Marie who God completely healed of Breast Cancer and is an Ambassador for American Cancer Society, inspirational speaker and author. Marie inspires so many people around the world to follow their dreams has also inspired me with writing my books and hosting my TV show, BeInspired Today.

Eric Williams, CEO of Thizz.TV and Out of The Box Productions has become a great friend, mentor and strategic partner. Eric is a renowned photo journalist and filmmaker. I am so blessed that God caused Eric to enter into my life at a critical time in my journey.

Beverly Kuykendall, V.P. of Corporate Growth Strategies for AvMedical LLC is a phenomenal business woman and friend.

I have known Beverly since elementary school and have watched her soar in her career as a Government Procurement specialist and keynote speaker. I am honored that she was one of my guests on my BeInspired Today TV show and has agreed to write the Forward to Faith Fuel for Your Journey.

Certificate of Registration

This Certificate issued under the seal of the Copyright
Office in accordance with title 17, *United States Code*,
attests that registration has been made for the work
identified below. The information on this certificate has
been made a part of the Copyright Office records.

Shira Perlmutter

United States Register of Copyrights and Director

Registration Number

TXu 2-318-136

Effective Date of Registration:
May 05, 2022
Registration Decision Date:
May 27, 2022

Title

Title of Work: Faith Fuel for Your Journey

Completion/Publication

Year of Completion: 2022

Author

Author: Clifford Frideric Wright
Author Created: text, artwork
Work made for hire: No
Citizen of: United States
Year Born: 1954

Copyright Claimant

Copyright Claimant: Clifford Frideric Wright
286 S. Poplar Ave., Apartment 12, Brea, CA, 92821, United States

Rights and Permissions

Name: Clifford Frideric Wright
Email: cliffwrightspeaks@gmail.com
Telephone: (951)258-1479
Alt. Telephone: (951)258-1852

Certification

Name: Clifford Frideric Wright
Date: May 05, 2022

14

CONTENTS

ENDORSEMENTS
Page 2

DEDICATION
Page 5

SPECIAL THANKS
Page 6

SPECIAL ACKNOWLEDGMENTS
Page 11

INTRODUCTION
Page 17

CHAPTER 1- Why is Faith So Important to Your Journey?
Page 24

CHAPTER 2- You Were Born On the Road to Your Personal Journey
Page 36

CHAPTER 3- Overcoming Fear Strengthens your Faith
Page 64

CHAPTER 4- The Power in Speaking Faith-Filled Words
Page 93

CHAPTER 5- The Power of Faith-Filled Prayers
Page 110

CHAPTER 6- Think on Positive Outcomes
Page 124

CHAPTER 7- Unscheduled Appointments
Page 138

INTRODUCTION

I was inspired to write and publish my second book, *Faith Fuel for Your Journey* about a month or two before the historic Coronavirus Pandemic in 2020. I could not have previously known that this divine theme would be so appropriate and needed during these turbulent times. In fact, my spirit was overwhelmed with the need to have *faith* for my own journey as I would later realize why. I will share more about that part of my journey later in this chapter.

My inspiration for writing about the revelation I received about the power and blessing of accessing *Faith Fuel for your Journey* jump started in December 2019. It was at an advisory board meeting I arranged for Orange County School District, Automotive Technology teachers, which was comprised of panelists from the automotive technology industry. During a question and answer session, one of the automotive teachers did something that was unusual for a meeting of this type. He stood up and told a heart-warming story, which was more like he was giving a testimony in church. As soon as he started telling the story, my spiritual antenna went up.

He began by telling the panel why it was important for students to be motivated in school and what seemed like a chance encounter transformed his bored students into enthusiastic ones.

Here is what the teacher said happened. One sweltering hot day, a woman with a one year-old toddler in the car seat, was driving when her radiator ran too hot. What made matters worse, she was stranded with no diapers to change her crying baby. This is when *Faith Fuel* intervened. Some of the automotive students happened to see the lady and her baby stranded in her car a few blocks away from their school. These board students rose to the occasion and pushed her car to the school's automotive repair shop and classroom. After inspecting her vehicle, the teacher told this woman in despair that she needed a new radiator. Not only did she not have the money for a radiator and her baby was crying, she was seeking a new job. In spite of her refusal, the teacher offered to pay for the radiator out his pocket. Although she did not know it, this is what I call God's love for her being demonstrated in action. He provided *Faith Fuel* for this lady to continue her *Journey*.

Not long after getting her new radiator, this same lady was blessed with a new job. One Saturday morning, the lady showed up with donuts for the students and teachers. She continued to do this every Saturday. The students got so inspired that they asked the instructor to let them start a program to offer low cost or free services to low income residents in the neighborhood. The school's principal was so impressed with how the students' attitude and grades improved that funding for their venture was approved. Now every Saturday morning, low income residents line up for blocks to get their cars serviced by these same students who were once bored out of their minds. They were changed into students who were now enthusiastic and passionate about going into automotive technology careers. The program became so successful that a local television news station and a local newspaper reported on this phenomenal story. The moral of this story is that when you find yourself in a situation where it appears that you are out of resources to continue on your journey, God has *Faith Fuel* for you to continue driving in the direction of your vision.

More importantly, like the lady that needed the radiator, God will use you to pay the blessing forward to help others and possibly make a monumental impact within your community.

The day after the advisory meeting, my wife, Sondria and I along with Pastors Keithalan and Maral Hinson and the Purpose Place Church LA family served breakfast to families who live in a homeless shelter. Pastor Keithalan, not knowing that I would hear this story, previously asked me to share a word of encouragement with the parents, who were single mothers. Most had several children.

I was impacted by the story about how God used the students and automotive teacher as *Faith Fuel* for the lady stranded in her car. I shared this inspirational story with these mothers. Afterward, many of the women told me they were truly inspired and received renewed hope. Their response confirmed that I was to write this book, *Faith Fuel for Your Journey*. I hope it encourages you and your family as well.

When I first started what I consider the most important book I have penned, unbeknown to me, governments around the whole world, including China, Italy, Korea, and the United States would need to quarantine billions of people in order to slow the spread of the Coronavirus in order to save as many lives as possible.

I could have never imagined that I, too, would need *Faith Fuel* for my own journey. I was one of millions of Americans who would be laid off from their job and later test positive for Covid 19. On many days during the most trying time of my life, I could have run out of *faith*. I thank God that He caused me to not die, but live and declare His works (**Psalm 118:17**). For me, *Faith Fuel for Your Journey* is not just a concept, it is real life. I realize, without God's grace, mercy and *Faith Fuel,* which includes my wife, Sondria tirelessly taking care of me, my children, Driana, Jy and Cliff II and extended family praying for me, I could have been one of the more than a half million people who died from Coronavirus. I realize now why God gave me an unrelenting burden to write and publish my most important piece of literary work, *Faith Fuel for Your Journey*. My desire is that by reading this God-inspired book, your *faith* is built so strongly that fear cannot have a place in your heart.

I pray that during this most troublesome time that you obtain peace in the storm. That peace or *Faith Fuel* penetrates your heart from knowing that God's thoughts toward you are good, not evil and that He has a {good} hope and {prosperous} future for you and your family (**Jeremiah 29:11**).

You can trust God. He will always show up with a measure of *faith* before you run out. I am a living witness! Although my *faith* was tested during my battle with the Coronavirus, God guided me to the right place at the right time. He continuously filled me up with enough *faith* to continue on my journey. There were days that I thought I would not be here but, the Lord showed me He is not finished with me yet. He kept His promise that He will complete what He started in my life. The fact that you are reading this book, He is doing the same for you.

My burning desire and conviction to writing *Faith Fuel for Your Journey* has taken on a new meaning. I am so thankful that the Lord saved my life and I must share it with you and others who may be going through a trial in their *faith*. As I am writing it, the World is still going through a horrific event that will be in the history books. Movies will be produced about it- the Coronavirus or Covid 19.

Especially now, people of all races and ethnic groups around the world need *Faith Fuel* for the rest of their journey. I pray that the words that God has inspired me to write, fills your heart with *faith*, hope and courage to continue on the road that leads to your purpose in life. More than ever you and I need *faith fuel* to get to the next pit stop in our lives. The Good News is this fuel is free!

You don't have to worry about the price of *Faith Fuel* going up. It has already been paid for by our Lord and Savior, Jesus Christ! To those who have not received Christ into your heart, God wants to pay for your fuel. You don't have to pay for it yourself!

CHAPTER ONE

Why is Faith So Important to Your Journey?

Faith is like gasoline or fuel for your car. It enables you to keep traveling on your journey road in pursuit of your dreams and visions. Just like you cannot drive your car without fuel, neither can you get very far in life without this most important substance called *faith*.

Can you imagine taking a cross country road trip with family without stopping to fill your car with gasoline every few hundred miles? Of course not! My wife bought me a decal for the wall in my office that says, "Life is a journey, not a destination". If that statement is true, then *faith* for your journey is as important as gasoline is for your car.

During one of Jesus' many conversations with Peter, He told him that He would pray that his *faith* would not fail him during one of Peter's most challenging times (**Luke 22:32**). He even told Peter the cock would crow three times and he would deny Him before men. Jesus knew that this sometimes temperamental disciple would cave into fear to the point he would deny Him three different times. Peter, even uttered a few choice cuss words to cover up his relationship with the Chosen one.

The fact that Jesus specifically prayed for Peter's *faith* to be in full effect, is a humongous clue of how important *faith* is to our journey. Our Lord and Savior foreknew that Peter, who sometimes did wrong things without thinking about his actions first, would one day run out of *faith yet,* knew Peter would eventually complete his journey and do great works for the Kingdom of God. However, during the process he would need to have *Faith Fuel* to continue in his ministry.

How about the woman with the issue of blood? For twelve years she lived with this awful condition. But she said to herself, "If I can just get to Jesus to touch the hem of His garment, I will be healed". In fact, out of all the masses that touched Him, Jesus felt His healing virtue go out of Him when the woman touched His robe. He told her "Daughter your *faith* has made you whole" **(Matthew 5:25-34).**

When we are driving along in life with minimal opposition, our *faith* is strong. It is when we figuratively run into bumps in the road, that we want reassurance that we will make it to our destination safely, especially when we are traveling long distances. We are conscious of how much gasoline we have in our tank. This scenario is also true in real life.

The longer it takes for us to accomplish our goals, the more we pay attention to whether we have enough *faith* to get us there.

As I shared earlier, you can compare your journey to more of a family road trip than a drive across town. It takes more gas to drive across the country than it does to drive within the city. You will need to fill your tank more frequently when driving a long distance than you would when driving to and from work or going shopping. This same equation applies to your *faith*. It typically requires more *faith* for choosing who you are going to marry, purchase a home or believing for healing in your body than it does for simpler things in life.

Now that we have established the importance and the power of having *faith fuel for your journey*, let's look at Biblical answers to the following questions to set on you on the right course.

1. **How Much Faith Do You Need?**
2. **How Do You Obtain Faith?**

How Much Faith Do You Need?

Unlike knowing how many gallons of gas you need to fill up your gas tank, the quality of your *faith* is more important than the size of your *faith.* Jesus said "Truly, if you have *faith* the size of a grain of a mustard seed (which is the smallest seed in the world) you can move mountains and nothing will be impossible to you (**Matthew 17:20**).

God foreknew how much faith you would need in your life. **Romans 12:3**, "For I say, through the grace given to me, to everyone who is among you, not to think of himself more highly than he ought to think, but to think soberly, as God has dealt to each one a measure of *faith*.

When you think of the size or quality of your own *faith*, it can be quite daunting. On the contrary, when you put your faith in God, it gives you peace of mind. You know the Lord's *faith* will never run out.

The following scriptures should set your mind at ease when you are at a juncture on your journey where the vision you are believing God for seems to be far off:

- **Habakkuk 2:2-4,** "Then the Lord answered me and said, write the vision and make it plain on tablets, that he may run who reads it. For the vision is for an appointed time; but at the end it will speak and it will not lie. Though it tarries, wait for it; because it will surely come. It will not tarry. Behold the proud, his soul is not upright in him; "but the just shall live by His *faith*".

- **Galatians 3:11,** "But that no one is justified by the law in the sight of God is evident for the just shall live by *faith*."

These two scriptures further validate how essential *faith* is in pursuit of your purpose. Each one says the just shall *live* by *faith*. This is Good News! These phrases let you know that if you are *just* (one who has received Christ as your Lord and Savior) you will *live* and function because of His *faith*.

Have Faith in God

Just like the quality of your gasoline depends on the oil company you purchase it from, so is your *faith* in God. When the disciples saw that the fig tree had dried up after Jesus cursed it, they were astonished. Here is what Jesus said about *faith*. "Have *faith* in God. For assuredly, I say to you, whoever says to this mountain, be removed and be cast into the sea, and does not doubt in his heart, but believes that those things he says will be done, he will have whatsoever he says. Therefore, I say to you, when you pray, believe that you receive them and you will have them" **(Mark 11:22-24)**.

Cheap gasoline will cause your vehicle to run poorly. To make sure you don't junk up your *faith*, **Mark 11:25-26** says, "And whenever you stand praying, if you have anything against anyone, forgive him, that your Father in Heaven may also forgive you your trespasses. But if you do not forgive, neither will your Father in Heaven forgive your trespasses." During your road trip or journey, you might find the family may become irritated with each other, so it is critical that you decide before leaving, to forgive each other regardless of what happens along the way.

In the summer of 1995, my first cousins and I drove from Southern California to my hometown, Tyler, Texas to attend our grandmother's funeral. We had fun and laughter, but we had to contend with the sun blazing, hot weather and my cousin's car stopping a few times, we had some heated arguments, Lol.

Like any parent, you want your family to enjoy your road trip together. It is supposed to be a time for you to have conversations and laughter. Prepare yourself. There will be things you cannot control. Depending on the season you are traveling, the weather will be extremely hot or very cold. Along the way, you will need to stop to use the restrooms, which may or may not be clean. No matter how healthy you eat, eventually you will eat some fast food. Needless to say, all these conditions lead to some uncomfortable times during the trip. Spiritually speaking, there will be times during your life's journey that will be less than favorable. However, your *faith* in God will strengthen you and keep you on the road to your desired destination. This leads me to question number two. How do you obtain *faith*?

How Do You Obtain Faith?

Unlike paying for fuel at a gas station, *faith fuel* is free of charge. All you have to do is open your spiritual ears. Faith comes by consistently hearing the Word of God (**Romans 10:17**). Hearing with your spiritual ears is key to obtaining *faith*. God will speak to you through your inner voice, mind and heart. As you are traveling on your journey, He will lead and guide you into all truth through the Holy Spirit **(John 16:13).** The more you spend time in God's presence and praying in the spirit, you will be able to discern His voice. Knowing when He is speaking to you will give you a sense of peace when you need it the most.

When my daughter, Driana was a freshman in college, she spent one semester in England. One Sunday afternoon after church, I was taking a nap. The Lord woke me up saying, "your daughter is in trouble". He said don't tell your wife and son what I am telling you. *She would have panicked*. But get them together and pray in tongues. Not long after we finished praying, Driana called and said, "I first want you to know I am okay." She went on to explain that she and a couple of her classmates, were in Paris, France visiting for the weekend. They had rented a cabin in a camp site.

She said she was laying down on the bed, and suddenly felt an urge to switch positions. She placed her head at the opposite end of the bed. Within seconds, a man busted the window, which was right above her. Had she not switched her position, the shattered glass would have been on her face instead of her feet, which were under the cover. Not only did she not get a scratch on her, she raised up, rebuked the man in the name of Jesus and he ran away! Driana prayed with her crying friends and reported the incident to the camp managers. Thank God, the police caught and arrested the man as he was breaking into another cabin of young ladies. Not only did hearing God's voice *fuel my faith*, but it also *fueled* my daughter's *faith* for her journey. Here she was on the other side of the Earth yet God provided *faith fuel* for our journey forever.

Now that we have answered the questions of how much *faith* do you need and how do you obtain *faith,* let's drive further down the journey highway.

Review of Chapter One

To make sure you have enough *faith fuel* to make it to the next station, Chapter 2, let's review a few highlights from Chapter 1.

A. Why is Faith Important to Your Journey?

- During one of Jesus' many conversations with Peter, He told him that He would pray that his *faith* would not fail him during one of Peter's most challenging times (**Luke 22:32**).

- The fact that Jesus specifically prayed for Peter's *faith* to be in full effect, is a giant clue of how important *faith* is to our journey.

B. How Much Faith Do You Need To Have?

- Unlike knowing how many gallons of gas you need to fill your gas tank, the quality of your *faith* is more important than the size of your *faith*. Jesus said "Truly, if you have *faith* the size of a grain of a mustard seed, *which is the smallest seed in the world*, you can move mountains and nothing will be impossible to you (**Matthew 17:20**)."

C. Have Faith in God

- Just like the quality of your gasoline depends on the oil company you purchase it from, so is your *faith* in God. When the disciples saw the fig tree dried up after Jesus cursed it, they were astonished. Here is what Jesus said about *faith*. "Have *faith* in God.

For assuredly, I say to you, whoever says to this mountain, be removed and be cast into the sea, and does not doubt in his heart, but believes that those things he says will be done, he will have whatsoever he says. Therefore, I say to you, when you pray, believe that you receive them and you will have them" (**Mark 11:22-24**)."

D. How Do You Obtain Faith?

- All you have to do is open your spiritual ears. Faith comes by consistently hearing the Word of God (**Romans 10:17**). Hearing with your spiritual ears is the key to obtaining *faith*.

CHAPTER TWO

You Were Born On the Road

to Your Personal Journey

The moment you and I were born we were put on the road to our personal journey. We all will need *Faith Fuel* to get to our desired destination. Again, your life journey can be likened to a cross country road trip. In God's sovereign will, He gave us a starting place in which we had no choice in the matter. None of us were able to choose our parents, ethnicity, race or place of birth. As much as I would relish the opportunity to make some changes at the beginning of my life, one thing I am grateful for and would not change is that I was born in America. Even though our country is plagued with the disease called racism and has to battle gun violence, millions of people around the world wish they were born here. I know we have a lot of inequities in this country, but we have an opportunity to level the playing field. It may not be easy, but it is possible! In other words, you will need *faith* for the long haul!

This leads me to share the following scriptures that will fill you with *Faith Fuel for Your Journey*:

- **Hebrews 10:35-39**, (35) "Therefore do not cast away your confidence, which has great reward." (36) "For *after* you have done the Will of God, you may receive the promise." (37) "For yet a little while, and He who is coming will come and will not tarry (wait)." (38) "Now the just shall live (one day at a time) by *faith*; but if anyone draws back, My soul has no pleasure in him."

- **James 1:19,** "Blessed is the man who endures temptation; for when he has been approved, he will receive the crown of life which the Lord has promised to those who love Him."

After decades of believing God for breakthroughs in our lives, my wife and I are finally experiencing some of the blessings we had been praying for and walking by *faith* to obtain them. There were many times when we thought our *faith* would run out.

Like most people, I wish I was born into a family unit where the father and mother remained married until death do they parted, owned a house with a white picket fence, and had plenty of money in the bank.

However, that was not how my journey started. Conversely, my parents got a divorce when I was a year and a half. When I was five years old my little brother was born. His father chose not to raise him either. Even though I was in kindergarten, my life's journey was off to a bumpy start, which included us having to move more than ten times by the time I was eight years old.

I wish I could tell you that the road to my destiny has been smooth. That would be a lie. What I can tell you is my mother was a trail blazer and had amazing faith. She moved our family from our hometown, Tyler, Texas to Los Angeles, California in the early '60s. Because of Willie Nell Wright's example, I have been able to grab ahold of faith during my journey. I can honestly say my mother's courageous step of *faith* forever changed the course of my life's journey. If it was not for her belief that God had a better life for us in Los Angeles, I would not have met and married the mother of my children. I am sure you can look back over your life and see how your parents' acts of faith set you on the course of your life. I can still remember the long drive from Texas to Los Angeles. Although our trip took about three days, it seemed like forever.

I also remember the road trips back to Texas when we would visit our grandparents during the summer.

Whether we were traveling to or from Los Angeles or Texas, each trip required that we stopped to fill the tank with gasoline. The same is true for our lives; we need fuel for our journey-*Faith Fuel*.

Faith Fuel Pumps are Close By

Over the years, my wife and I have taken our children and grandson on cross country road trips. Along the way, the fuel gauge signals the importance of reading the road signs that show the number of miles to the next gas station. Usually, the gas stations are within a relatively short distance from each other so that you don't run out of gas. Often, our lives are like that fuel gauge in our car. It alerts you when you are running out of *Faith Fuel*. The Good News (The Gospel), is there is a filling station close by and the gas is free! Those who don't believe in Christ are living their lives like a traveler driving a car that is running on empty and has no money to fill it with gas.

No one in their right mind would drive their car across country without having enough money to buy gasoline. However, these days it is not uncommon for you to be approached by a stranger asking for money to buy gas.

Unfortunately, most people can only afford to help a stranded person with a dollar or two. Even if that traveler is fortunate enough to receive enough money to fill their tank, it is highly unlikely they would reach their destination if they depend on others to give them gas money for their entire trip. However, if this same traveler were blessed enough to pull into gas stations where the owner of the stations were giving everyone free gas, that would be a miracle. For your information, our God who owns all the silver and gold on a thousand hills and all that dwell on the Earth, also owns all the *Faith Fuel Pumps* and will give you *Faith Fuel for Your Journey, free of charge*!

Those who planned the infrastructure of our roads system in America knew beforehand people who travel by car would need to buy gas every so many miles in order to get to their destination. They also knew they would need to stop to use the restrooms and buy food and beverages.

If mere men knew these factors would be required, how much more would your Heavenly Father plan to get you to your desired location? He knew beforehand which route you would take and made sure it leads to the place where His purpose for your life is fulfilled. Along your way, the Master planner provides *Faith Fuel for Your Journey*.

Late at night, on one of our last cross-country road trips, I was looking for a gas station. It was so dark that I mistakenly exited the highway onto a one lane, dirt road. Since I could not put the car in reverse to get back on the highway, I had no choice but to keep driving ahead by *faith*. All the while, I was praying under my breath so I did not frighten my wife and grandson, Michael. As I kept driving, low and behold bright lights to a gas station appeared ahead. I Praise God, I did not have to rely on my own *faith* to get us to the next gas station. It was if God led me to drive down that dark dirt road to show me He will always lead and guide me to a safe place. All I have to do is trust Him and walk by His *faith*. I would not be surprised if you had situations where you got on a dark path but God redirected you back to the light.

If you find yourself in a situation where you have gotten off track and it is too late to turn around and go the other way, keep trusting in God and move ahead in His *faith*.

I hope you find the following scripture to be comforting. It encourages you to move forward in confidence. **Philippians 3:12-14,** Paul wrote, Not that I have already attained, or am already perfected; but I press on, that I may lay hold of that for which Christ Jesus has also laid hold of me. (Verse 13), Brethren, I do not count myself to have apprehended; but one thing I do, forgetting those things which are behind and reaching forward to those things which are ahead. (Verse 14), I press toward the goal for the prize of the upward call of God in Christ Jesus.

What a Difference a Day Makes

A few years ago, the Lord inspired me to write this quote, "Today is a day you have never seen before, and will never see again. So take full advantage of it". It reminds me of the scripture, **Psalm 118:24**, "This is the day that the Lord has made, I will rejoice and be glad in it." This scripture is often quoted by many Christians without giving it much thought. It became Rhema (tattooed on my heart) to me about 15 years ago when I attended a service at Zoe Christian Fellowship of Whittier, where the late, Dr. Myles Monroe spoke. He made the statement "Never underestimate the value of one day." His words still resonate with me to this day.

There have been many times I had a difficult decision to make. Rather than worry, I learned to just go to sleep. Usually, the Lord gives me my answer in a dream or vision while I am asleep. Sometimes, He will show me what I need to do the next morning, after I am fully rested. If you don't get anything else out of *Faith Fuel for Your Journey* apply this to your life-go to sleep when facing a difficult decision.

During the 2020 Olympic Games in Japan, Jade Carey failed in a vault the night before winning the gold medal in the all-around individual competition. When they interviewed her, the reporter asked Jade how it felt to win the Gold Medal after failing in one event the day before. Her answer was "My victory felt so much better and it seemed like it was supposed to happen that way." She added, "Having my dad as her coach made all the difference in the world." Likewise, having the Heavenly Father as your coach and comforter will cause your *faith* to rise even if you recently failed. There was a news photo of Jade's dad consoling and hugging her on the night she failed and another photo of him hugging and congratulating her on winning the gold medal. Both photos show her crying-one tears of sadness and the other tears of joy.

The following scriptures imply that we live one day at a time and that is how our *faith* works-one day at a time:

- **Matthew 6:34** 'Jesus tells the disciples, Therefore, do not worry about tomorrow, for tomorrow will worry about its own things. Sufficient for the day is its own trouble.
- **Romans 1:17** "The righteousness of God is revealed from *faith* to *faith*". As it is written in **Habakkuk 2:4**, "The just shall live by His *faith*."
- **2 Corinthians 5:7** "For we walk by *faith* and not by sight" implies that *faith* is exhibited one step at a time.

These are not just words on a page. They emulate life! Let these words of *faith* take residence in your heart and you will see some profound blessings. One of those blessings is divine insight which leads to peace.

One Saturday morning, my son, Jy and I went hiking on a trail that was surrounded by weeds and bushes. We were having a conversation about being a trailblazer. As we kept walking, I took photos of the trail. I then realized there were lilies surrounded by the weeds and bushes.

This experience was so powerful because it fit into my message I was to preach the next day, which was Father's Day. In my notes, I had previously edited out **Matthew 6:28**, "So why do you worry? Consider the lilies in the field, how they grow; they neither toil nor spin.

The Lord really got my attention in this one verse. He made me realize, He can cause us to grow and blossom in the midst of trouble. He wants you and I to know, there is nothing that can prevent us from excelling in life. He wants us to know we can prosper in any environment.

The next day, I preached my Father's Day message, "A Good Father Knows" with a fresh perspective on what it means to cast all your cares on your Heavenly Father. I encourage you to read and meditate on **Matthew 6:24-34**. It will strengthen your *faith* tremendously as you continue on your journey.

Faith Fuel to Fulfill Your Purpose

The age-old question is why, were you born. That question has entered the mind of most people. At some point in your life, usually around the age of six of seven, you begin to imagine what you will be when you grow up. Typically, by the time you are in your early teens, you began to take steps in the direction you are passionate about. Usually in your late teens is when you begin dating and thinking about who you would marry and have children with. When your children are born is when you realize you better find your purpose for your life-if you hadn't already.

That is when finding out why you were born and your pursuit of purpose becomes the most important thing in your life. During this time when you find out you need *Faith Fuel* to get to the place in your life where you find these answers and accomplish them.

The longer I live the more I study the Bible and observe the life of others. God's purpose for my life is to make a positive impact in the lives of the people He brings into my life, especially my family. You are no exception. God intends for you to think and live in such a way that people who are lost will be drawn to Him. This is what I call the *impact mindset*.

You may be asking yourself what is the *impact mindset*? Let me explain it this way. We all impact the lives of others, whether it is good or bad, especially our family and loved-ones. No matter if you are married or single, have children or not or have siblings or not, you have and will at some point in your life impact the life of another person or group of people. Your impact can be either positive or negative. Having an *impact mindset* involves intentionally living your life in such a way that will influence the people within your circle. I believe most of us want to make a positive impact on the lives of those who God places in our lives. In order to accomplish this over your lifetime, it will require *Faith Fuel*, especially when it involves being kind to people who treat you badly or indifferent. This is what I am going to call *Faith Fuel for Forgiveness*.

Faith Fuel to Forgive

Even the disciple Peter had a hard time embracing and exhibiting this most precious behavioral quality. In **Matthew 18:21**, he asked Jesus how many times he must forgive a brother (or sister) who sins against him. Jesus answered saying seven times seventy (in a day). Jesus went on to tell him a parable about a man who owed a huge debt to another man and he went to him and asked for forgiveness of that debt. After he was forgiven of the debt, he saw another man who owed him a small debt. The man asked for forgiveness. Although he was forgiven of the large debt, he refused to forgive the man who owed him a small debt. This resulted in the judge reminding him about the large debt he was forgiven of and being punished severely for not offering forgiveness to the man who owed him a smaller debt. This parable is a type and shadow of Jesus Christ, Who was crucified so that we would receive forgiveness of our sins. Through this parable, God wants us to realize the size of the sins we were forgiven of is huge compared to the offenses we incur during our lifetime. In order to offer forgiveness to someone who hurt you or even to forgive yourself of past sins, you cannot do it in your own strength- it takes the *Faith Fuel* to empower you to do that.

One of the reasons it is so difficult to forgive someone, especially your spouse, significant other, parents, siblings or even your children, is you are afraid that forgiving them may give them license to disappoint you again. Forgiveness requires bravery most of us don't have. It can be very illusive. One day you will feel like you have forgiven and then something causes you to remember what they did. In these instances, it stirs hurt or anger in you and causes you to feel like you did when the offense first happened. That is another reason why you need *Faith Fuel* to get you to the place in your heart and mind where God's peace replaces the anguish that accompanies the memory of the violation that interrupted the trust. The same is true whether you were the victim or perpetrator, you need *Faith Fuel* to empower you to maintain the right mindset.

Here are some scriptures that can help you fill up your *Faith Fuel* tank:

- **Phil: 4:8-9** " Finally brothers (sisters too), whatsoever things are true, whatsoever things are noble, whatsoever things are just, whatsoever things are pure, whatsoever things are lovely, whatsoever things are of a food report, if there be any virtue and if there is anything praiseworthy, meditate on these things. (Verse 9) The things which you learned and received and heard and saw in me, these do, and the God of peace will be with you.

- **Mark 11:25-26** "And whenever you stand praying, if you have anything against anyone, forgive him, so that your Father in Heaven may also forgive you, your trespasses. But if you do not forgive, neither will your Father in Heaven forgive your trespasses".

As I stated earlier, the previous scripture can be likened to putting cheap gas in your gas tank. Holding onto unforgiveness can clog up your *faith fuel.* It can cause your journey to be sluggish, harder and longer than it needs to be.

Even the Lord's Prayer, **Matthew 6:9-14** warns us to forgive those who trespass against us so that our Heavenly Father will forgive us of our own trespasses. Now that you have acknowledged how important forgiveness is to your *faith*, let's talk about forgiving yourself. Sometimes it is easier to forgive others than it is to forgive yourself. I know that has been true in my life.

Forgiving Yourself
Strengthens your Faith

While you are on your life journey, the enemy will remind you of your sins and mistakes no matter how long ago they were. The Bible says he is an accuser of the brethren before God day and night. Although he is the one who tempts you to sin, he is also the one who tries to condemn you for acting on his diabolical thoughts.

Thank God, He does not remember our sins once we have confessed them and received Christ as our Lord and Savior.

The following scriptures validate that your Heavenly Father is a forgiving Master:

> **Isaiah 43:25-28, "**I even I, am He who blots out your transgressions for My own sake. And I will not remember your sins. Put me in remembrance; Let us contend together; State your case, that you may be acquitted."

> **Isaiah 43:18,** "Do not remember the former things, Nor consider the things of old. Behold, I will do a new thing. Now it shall spring forth; shall you not know it? I will even make a road in the wilderness and rivers in the desert."

> **Micah 7:19,** "He will again have compassion on us. And will subdue our iniquities. You will cast all our sins to the depths of the sea."

The closer you get to achieving what God placed you on this Earth to do, the more frequently Satan will try to remind you of your past sins and failures to sabotage your journey. However, God has already gone before him to set the record straight.

There is no condemnation to those who are in Christ Jesus, **Romans 8:1**.

The devil will try to make you feel unworthy to receive God's blessings, favor and forgiveness. But even in the court of law, the prosecutors are not allowed to charge a defendant for the same crime for which they have already been exonerated. When the liar, Satan accuses you through your own thoughts or words of others, remind yourself that God does not remember your past. The only thoughts He has toward you are good and not evil and to give you a good hope and future, **Jeremiah 29:11**.

Forgiving yourself is not easy. It takes work and requires renewing your mind (**Romans 12:2**). Even after getting saved, for years I had trouble of forgiving myself for my past sins. As a new Christian, I was constantly at the altar. I remember one of my pastors at the time gave me a look like he was asking, you are up here again? I believe the condemnation I constantly dealt with slowed my growth. As I am writing these words, the Lord is revealing to me that forgiving yourself is the major part of obtaining and sustaining *Faith Fuel for Your Journey*. I thank God that He finally convinced me that when He looks at me, He only sees His Only Begotten Son, Jesus Christ.

My prayer is, as you are reading this, you too are released from the prison of condemnation and walk in your new-found freedom! Be sure to proceed to **Review of Chapter 2** before moving onto Chapter 3, in which we will discuss how overcoming fear to help you access *Faith Fuel for your Journey.*

Review of Chapter Two

Let's review some highlights of Chapter 2.

A. **You Were Born On the Road to Your Personal Journey**

- In God's sovereign will, He gave us a starting place, from which we had no choice in the matter. None of us were able to choose our parents, ethnicity, race or place of birth.

- **Hebrews 10:35-36**, (35) "Therefore do not cast away your confidence, which has great reward". (36) "For *after* you have done the Will of God, you may receive the promise."

B. Faith Fuel Pumps are Close By

- Often, our lives are like the fuel gauge in our car. It alerts you when you are running out of *Faith Fuel*. The Good News (The Gospel) is there is a filling (gas) station close by and the gas is free!

- I hope you find the following scripture to be very comforting. It encourages you to move forward in confidence. **Philippians 3:12-14,** Paul wrote, Not that I have already attained, or am already perfected; but I press on, that I may lay hold of that for which Christ Jesus has also laid hold of me. (Verse 13), Brethren, I do not count myself to have apprehended; but one thing I do, forgetting those things which are behind and reaching forward to those things which are ahead. (Verse 14), I press toward the goal for the prize of the upward call of God in Christ Jesus.

C.   What a Difference a Day Makes

- A few years ago, the Lord inspired me to write this quote, "Today is a day you have never seen before, and will never see again. So take full advantage of it". It reminds me of the scripture, **Psalm 118:24**, "This is the day that the Lord has made, I will rejoice and be glad in it".

- There have been many times I've had a difficult decision to make. Rather than worry, I have learned to just go to sleep. Usually, the Lord gives me my answer in a dream or vision while I am asleep. Or sometimes, He will show me what I need to do the next morning, after I am fully rested. If you don't get anything else out of my book, *Faith Fuel for Your Journey*, apply this to your life-go to sleep when you are facing a difficult decision.

D. Faith Fuel to Fulfill Your Purpose

- At some point in your life, especially when your children are born, you realize you better find your purpose for your life-if you hadn't already.

E. Faith Fuel to Forgive

- Even the disciple Peter had a hard time embracing and exhibiting this most precious behavioral quality. In **Matthew 18:21**, he asks Jesus how many times he must forgive a brother (or sister) who sins against him. Jesus answered saying seven times seventy (in a day). Jesus told a parable about a man who owed a larger debt to another man and he went to him and asked for forgiveness of that debt. After he was forgiven of the debt, he saw another man who owed him a small debt. That man asked for forgiveness.

Although he was forgiven of the large debt, he refused to forgive the man that owed him a small debt. The judge reminded him about the larger debt he was forgiven of and was punished severely for not offering forgiveness to the man who owed him a smaller debt. This parable is a type and shadow of Jesus Christ, Who was crucified so that we would receive forgiveness of our sins. Through this parable, God wants us to realize the size of the sins we were forgiven of is huge compared to the offenses we will incur during our lifetime. In order to offer forgiveness or forgive yourself of your past sins, you cannot do it in your own strength-it takes the *Faith Fuel* to empower you to do that.

F. Forgiving Yourself Strengthens your Faith

- While you are on your life journey, the enemy will remind you of your sins and mistakes no matter how long ago they were. The Bible says he is an accuser of the brethren before God day and night. Although he is the one who tempts you to sin, he is also the one who tries to condemn you for acting on his diabolical thoughts.

- Thank God, He does not remember our sins once we have confessed them and received Christ as our Lord and Savior.

The following scriptures validate that your Heavenly Father is a forgiving Master:

- **Isaiah 43:25-28, "**I even I am He who blots out your transgressions for My own sake. And I will not remember your sins. Put me in remembrance; Let us contend together; State your case, that you may be acquitted.
- **Isaiah 43:18,** "Do not remember the former things, Nor consider the things of old. Behold, I will do a new thing. Now it shall spring forth; shall you not know it? I will even make a road in the wilderness and rivers in the desert.
- **Micah 7:19,** "He will again have compassion on us. And will subdue our iniquities. You will cast all our sins to the depths of the sea".
- The closer you get to achieving what God put you on this Earth to do, the more frequently Satan will try to remind you of your past sins and failures to sabotage your journey.

However, God has already gone before him to set the record straight. There is no condemnation to those who are in Christ Jesus, **Romans 8:1**.

CHAPTER THREE

Overcoming Fear Strengthens your Faith

Like condemnation, the devil uses fear and intimidation to convince you to quit in the middle of your journey. I have heard it said that the key to overcoming fear is to meet the thing that fears you most head on. In other words, run toward the imaginary fearful thing.

When I was in the eighth grade, a bully in my classroom was telling jokes about my mother. I responded with some jokes about his mother. Lol, what did I do that for? This guy was a big thirteen year old. He could have been six feet and 200 hundred pounds. Mind you, at that time, I was only about 5'1 and 104 pounds. When he told me in front of the whole class that he was going to beat me up after class was over, in my mind I was scared. However, righteous indignation came over me. I began to think about how he was the one who started talking about my mother first! The more I thought about it, the madder I became.

Before we left the classroom, I decided that I was going to face my giant. When I stood in front of him and told him I was ready to fight him, he looked at me as if I was crazy, which was daring since he was almost twice my size. I thank God that he uttered the words, "It's alright man. We don't have to fight". Whew, praise the Lord, lol!

The moral to the story is that running toward your fear catches the enemy off guard. Here are Biblical stories and scriptures that can strengthen you in overcoming fear that weakens *faith*.

2 Timothy 1:6-7, "Therefore, I remind you to stir up the gift of God which is in you through the laying on of hands." For God has not given us a spirit of fear, but of power and love and a sound mind." Notice the phrase *spirit of fear*. It implies that fear is a spirit. This scripture lets us know that God gave us a different set of spirits, *spirit of power, love and a sound mind*. The part of the verse I like most is that we have the right and option to reject the spirit of fear and choose to embrace the spirit of *power, love and a sound mind*. If fear clogs your *faith fuel*, you can choose not to mix it with your mindset.

I John 4:18, "There is no fear in love; but perfect love casts out fear, because fear involves torment. But he who fears has not been made perfect in love".

There are so many scriptures about fear that it is clear that God does not want it to be part of our lives. The two previous scriptures describe fear as a spirit that causes you not to use the gifts that God has given you. It causes torment. It has been said that fear is the opposite of *faith*. And it is impossible to please God without *faith* (**Hebrews 11:6**).

God Is With You on Your Journey

Another reason our Heavenly Father does not tolerate fear in His children is because He is with us every minute of the day. As a father, my feelings would be hurt if one of my children were to act fearful when I am with them. I would question haven't I shown you that I protected you from the day you were born? Well, our Heavenly Father feels the same. He constantly tells us in scriptures not to be fearful *because I am with you.*

One of the most well-known scriptures, The 23rd Psalms, certainly confirms that God is with you. **Psalm 23: 4** says "Yea though I walk through the shadow of death, I will fear no evil; for You are with me; Your rod and Your staff, they comfort me. Most parents teach this scripture to their children at a very young age, and rightfully so.

Last summer, I had an opportunity to be fearful. My wife and I were on a flight to visit our daughter. On the way, my blood pressure dropped causing me to pass out. When I came to, a passenger who was a nurse and flight attendants were attending to me. I had a peace in my spirit that I was going to be alright. In fact, I was able to walk off the plane without any assistance. As a precaution, I was taken to the ER at a local hospital.

They ran all kinds of tests: an EKG, a brain scan, blood test, lung check, and a stress text. They discovered was I was taking too much blood pressure medication. The doctors told me to stop taking one of the two blood pressure medications I was on. I knew God was with me all the while. I had peace and did not have fear something was seriously wrong with my health.

My blood pressure has been normal ever since and my doctor has instructed me to take half the dosage of the one blood pressure medication. I encourage you to look for God in every situation you find yourself in.

When You Look For God in Every Situation You Will Find Him

While visiting our daughter in New York, I went on a morning walk at a beautiful park across the street from her apartment. I found about ten flights of stairs that I was inspired to walk up. Once I got to the top of the stairs, there was this breathtaking scenery that overlooked New York City. I had no idea what to expect while I was walking up the stairs. Had I quit on the way up, as I was tempted to do, I would have missed out on this picturesque view of God's beauty.

Although my mind was telling me to stop, I am so glad that I continued in faith to walk those stairs. I found God in a way that I had never done before. I encourage you to continue seeking God in your everyday activities. He will reveal glorious things that you never expected. I pray that my story inspires you to "walk by faith and not by sight" (**2 Corinthians 5:7**).

There are moments and days when things happen that are not within your control. I am a living witness that when you earnestly seek to find God in every circumstance, you will receive an uncommon peace. You will gain a higher level of confidence that you did not previously have. I call this God-Fidence. In other words, your confidence is based on your trust in the love and power of God, not in your own ability. Knowing that your Heavenly Father is with you in unpredictable encounters, gives you *faith fuel* to press forward on your journey.

Faith Fuel to Have God-Fidence like Abraham

When God told Abram to leave his father's house and go to a land that He would show him, it took uncommon confidence (God-Fidence) to obey God and strike out on his own. Even though he did not have any children at the time, God promised to make Abram a great nation. He told him He would make his name great and that Abram would be a blessing. God decreed that He would bless Abram to be a blessing, bless those who blessed him and curse those who cursed him. If that wasn't enough, God told Abram that all the families of the Earth would be blessed through him.

After hearing those promises, Abram obeyed God and stepped out in *faith* and God-Fidence. As a result, we have Jesus Christ, our Lord and Savior. God made good on His promise. This story found in **Genesis 12:1-3**, was written to show you and me an example of blessings that come by obeying God and walking by faith even in the most seemingly impossible situations.

God Blessings Us Even When We Don't Deserve It

Abram, whose name was later changed to Abraham faced multiple roadblocks during his journey where he had to lean on his *faith* in God. The first roadblock was in his mind. He was seventy five years old, married to Sarai who was barren, and had to believe God's promise to give the land of Canaan to his descendants. Like what's happened to you and me when we stepped out on the vision God gave us, Abram and Sarai's journey, alike, took them through Egypt, a land of famine and to make matters worse, Abram took his nephew, Lot along, later proving to be a mistake.

Abram did not exhibit God-Fidence in this unexpected stop in Egypt. He feared for his life and told Sarai to lie to Pharaoh saying she was his sister. Even though Abram failed this test, God covered him with His protection, mercy and grace. Pharaoh recognized God's Hand of protection on Abram and Sarai. He blessed them with riches as they continued with their journey. The same is true for us when we have failed to exude God-Fidence and walk in our God-given authority-God blesses us even when we don't deserve it.

I used to wonder why God blessed my life so much even when I did not deserve it. I no longer beat myself up when I miss it. I have learned to accept that God told me I can come boldly to His throne of grace, so that I may obtain mercy and find grace to help in my time of need (**Hebrews 4:16**). If you feel like you don't deserve God's blessings, I encourage you to accept His free gift through Jesus Christ. Be honest, if you ran out of gas on your road trip and someone offered to pay for a full tank of gas, wouldn't you accept it? The good news is during your journey in life, no matter how good a person you may be, you cannot earn God's free gift of salvation.

All you have to do is accept it. **Ephesians 2:8-9** says, "For by grace you have been saved through faith, and that not of yourselves; it is the free gift of God. Not of works, lest anyone should boast".

If you have not yet received God's free gift of salvation, this is a good time to do so. Just speak from your heart the words found in **Romans 10:9-10, "**I confess Jesus Christ as the Lord of my life, and I believe in my heart that, Heavenly Father you raised Him from the dead. You said with my heart I believe in the righteousness through your Son, Christ Jesus. And with my mouth, my confession has been made to obtain salvation". I thank you Father God that I am now saved. Now fill me with your *faith* for my life's journey.

Be Sure To Enjoy the Scenery on Your Journey

On your life's road trip, be sure to enjoy the scenery along the way. Depending on where you are traveling from, you may see oceans, mountains, and even deserts. Either way, God will use every part of your trip for His glory. Not one stop or turn will be in vain. **Romans 8:28**, "And we know that all things work together for good to those who love God, to those who are called according to His purpose."

During the fall season, in some regions, the leaves turn multiple colors. If you allow God to speak to you, you will recognize He was very intentional in His creation. There are mountains, oceans and deserts, in California. West Texas is very different from South, North and East Texas. Cities like El Paso are pretty much desert. The weather is similar to New Mexico and Arizona. South, North and East Texas are on flat land and have a lot of trees and greenery. Houston, and Beaumont are closer to the Gulf of Mexico. As a result, they are subject to hurricanes much like New Orleans, Louisiana. Florida has warm weather like California. It is much more humid like Texas, New Orleans, Alabama, and Georgia. New York, Chicago and Detroit are known for their cold weather and snow. However, during the summer, they are very hot and humid.

On our visit to New York in July, 2021, we were met with heat, humidity and rain all on the same day. The point I am making is no matter where your journey may leads, there is purpose in every part of your trip.

You may remember on your family vacations and road trips, your parents pointing out sights that did not seem interesting to you. My wife and I have done that with our children and grandchildren. When you pass by your old high school or college, you enthusiastically tell stories to your children or grandchildren that bore them. The reason they are not excited is because they don't understand the value of your experience. Some adults are the same way. They don't understand or appreciate the value in what their Heavenly Father is trying to show them in His Word. They are oblivious to the beauty that is around them.

Several years ago, some posted a photo of a Jacaranda tree on a street that was lined with regular trees. The beautiful purple leaves stood out so much that I now appreciate seeing them as I am driving. My wife thinks I am corny because of my enthusiasm for these wonderful creations. There is a street in Whittier, California that is lined with these Jacaranda trees. It is truly a sight to see.

Sometimes I am driving on the freeway not conscious of the presence of these trees. Then all of a sudden the Lord quickens my mind and causes me to be aware that they are all around me. What a wonderful feeling it is to recognize God's creation.

You may ask yourself, what does admiring the scenery have to do with *having Faith Fuel for Your Journey*? That is a good question! The answer is *faith* comes in many different ways.

- It highlights how meticulous God is and how He pre-planned how the Earth would look so you and I would enjoy our journey.
- If God went through this much detail, His plan for you must be very important.
- Every one of God's creations has a purpose and so does your life.
- God knew you would need enjoyable experiences to bring balance to your journey.
- God will use every one of your journey experiences to prepare you for achieving your goals.

God Created the Earth for You to Enjoy On Your Journey

The first chapter of Genesis shows that God put a lot of thought into the creation of the Universe. He made sure that the Sun was perfectly set far enough away that we don't get burned up. The moon was positioned by our Creator to make sure it gives us enough light at night, yet not too close to cause us to freeze. He intentionally created the earth as the only planet that humans could live on. The first book and first chapter of the Bible shows us that our Creator intentionally created an atmosphere for us to live in and enjoy. **Genesis 1:1 and 2**, lets us know that God created everything out of nothing. "In the beginning God created the heavens and the earth." The earth was without form and void; and darkness was on the face of the deep. And the Spirit of God was hovering over the face of the waters".

I am so glad that the first thing He created was light to dispel darkness. The first thing I do in the morning is open the blinds and curtains to our windows and sliding glass door to our patio and thank the Lord for another day.

The sunlight is so energizing and refreshing. No wonder doctors recommend getting daily exposure to sunlight as a natural way to maintain good health. **Genesis 1:3-4** says, "Then God said, let there be light and there was light. And God saw the light that it was good; and God divided the light from the darkness. If God said the light is good-it is good! It reenergizes you and helps you see and appreciate the beauty God created for you along the way on your journey.

God's Plan for You Is Very Important to Him

I have too many times to count when I felt God left me stranded in the middle of my journey. But, He has always shown up and given me a spiritual jump to help me get back on the road to my journey. I recently had to travel for my job. Since my trip also involved some leisure time, I bought a plane ticket for Sondria to visit her aunt while I worked in a different city. The plan was for us to meet up in Houston, Texas to fly back home together. However, a monkey wrench was thrown into my itinerary. I received an alert that my flight to Houston would be delayed by an hour.

This meant I would arrive too late to join my wife on the flight home to Los Angeles. God knew this would cause a tremendous inconvenience and that it was important to me to be on the same flight home with my wife. He supernaturally intervened and caused my flight to land in Houston in one hour instead of an hour and a half. I had to walk very fast in order get to the gate leaving for Los Angeles.

All the passengers, including my wife, were on the plane about to take off. Thank God there was an agent still at the gate desk. When I explained my situation to him, he ran to the plane to ask them to allow me on the plane! Sondria was so surprised when she saw me on the plane, lol!

There are many scriptures that illustrate that God's plan for you is very important to Him. **Philippians 1:6**, "Being confident of this very thing, that He who began a good work in you will complete it until the day of Jesus Christ.

Hebrews 13:20-21, "Now may the God of peace who brought up our Lord Jesus from the dead, that great Shepherd of the sheep, through the blood of everlasting covenant, make you complete in every good work to do His will, working in you what is well pleasing in His sight, through Jesus Christ to whom glory forever and ever. Amen".

2 Timothy 3:16-17, "All scripture is given by inspiration of God, and is profitable for doctrine, for reproof, for correction, for instruction in righteousness, that the man of God may be complete thoroughly equipped for every good work."

Your Life's Journey Has a Purpose

As a young boy and now a 67 year old man, I have always wondered why certain things happened in my life. It seemed to me I never fit in, no matter where I went to school, lived, worked or even attended church. To this day, nothing has changed. No matter how hard I try, something happens that makes me realize I am different. I am sure you've had the same experience. Like me, you probably feel left out, ostracized, or rejected, even within your own family or neighborhood.

I finally came to the conclusion and accepted the fact that God set me apart because of the purpose He has for my life. Likewise, you may as well embrace the fact that you too are set apart for God's divine purpose for your life.

When my youngest son, Jy was growing up, I had to explain to him why he was different and help him to understand that not fitting in with his friends was God's way of preparing him for leadership. I used an analogy of him being a pilot and his friends being the passengers. I explained that it would be dangerous for him to step out of the cockpit to sit with his passengers. They would crash!

The same is true for you. You are the captain of your airplane of life. In order to land safely at your destination, you have to stay focused on your divine flight plan. As much as you would like to kick it with your passengers, those same people are depending on you to land the plane safely for everyone.

Here are scriptures and stories about the importance of staying on track to your purpose:

Mark 8:27- 33, Jesus had to rebuke Peter because he tried to tell Jesus He would not have to die. What Peter did not know was it was Jesus' sole purpose for being born so that He could save mankind from sin.

At the tender age of twelve, without His parent's permission, Jesus stayed behind three days in Jerusalem with the teachers listening and asking questions. When Mary and Joseph found Him and asked Jesus why He did such a thing, His response was, "Why have you sought me? Did you not know I must be about my Father's business?"   **(Luke   2:40-49)**

God Wants You to Have Balance on Your Journey

When you think of a journey, sometimes you can have the impression that it is going to be tedious and unenjoyable. While it is true you will have some difficult times as you are pursuing your life purpose, God also wants you to have pleasurable times.

That is why we have holidays like Thanksgiving, Christmas and Labor Day. Marriages, births and graduations were also created by God to bring enjoyment to your life. **Ecclesiastes 9:7**, "Go eat your bread with joy, and drink your wine with a merry heart (but don't get drunk), for God has already approved what you do."

Ecclesiastes 3:13, "Eat and drink and enjoy the fruits of your labor, for these are gifts from God."

Psalm 128:1-3, "Blessed is everyone who fears (references) the Lord, who walks in His ways. (2) When you eat the labor of your hands. You will be happy, and it shall be well with you. (3) Your wife shall be like a fruitful vine in the very heart of your house, your children like olive plants all around your table."

As I mentioned earlier, on my trip for work, I was able to experience some leisure. My first cousin, Tameka got married and Sondria and I were able to attend her wedding reception. Plus, I got to spend quality time with my aunt Freddie Mae and other cousins I had not seen in a few years. I even got to visit my hometown, Tyler, Texas on the same trip. God is truly good!

God Uses Every One of your Journey Experiences to prepare you for achieving your Goals

Like going to school, every class you take, such as Math prepares you for advanced subjects like Calculus and Geometry. God uses this same method to prepare you for more difficult stops on your life journey. Each mile of your journey can be likened to stepping up a ladder. Each step you take, positions you higher and higher. When you get to the top of the ladder, you are able to see things you could not see when you were on a lower rung. Below are scriptures that confirm how God uses every juncture in your life to mature you for the future:

I Corinthians 13:11, "When I was a child, I spoke as a child, I understood as a child, I thought as a child, but when I became a man, I put away childish things."

Hebrews 5:12- 14, "For though by this time you ought to be teachers, you need someone to teach you again the first principles of the oracles of God; and you have come to need milk and not solid food. (13) For everyone who partakes of only milk is unskilled in the Word of righteousness, for he is a babe.

(14) But solid food belongs to those who are of full age; that is those who by reason of use have their senses exercised to discern both good and evil."

I Peter 2:2, "As newborn babes, desire the pure milk of the Word, that you may grow thereby."

Essentially, these scriptures help us understand that our journey is a process and that we grow in every experience. *Having Faith Fuel on your Journey* helps you get to your destination. I encourage you to pray and embrace each step of your journey as God's way of fine tuning you to be one of His instruments.

Review of Chapter Three

Let's review highlights from Chapter 3.

A. Overcoming Fear Strengthens your Faith

- Like condemnation, the devil uses fear and intimidation to convince you to quit in the middle of your journey. I have heard it said that the key to overcoming fear is to meet the thing that fears you the most head on. In other words, run toward the imaginary fearful thing.

- Here are Biblical stories and scriptures that will strengthen you in overcoming fear that weakens your *faith*.

- **2 Timothy 1:6-7, "**Therefore, I remind you to stir up the gift of God which is you through the laying on of hands". "For God has not given us a spirit of fear, but of power and love and a sound mind. Notice the phrase, *spirit of fear*. It implies that fear is a spirit. This scripture lets you and I know that God gave us a different set of *spirits- power, love and a sound mind*. The part of the verse I like most is that we have the right and option to reject the *spirit of fear* and choose to embrace the spirit of *power, love and a sound mind*. If fear clogs your *faith fuel*, you can choose not to mix it in with your mindset.
- **I John 4:18**, There is no fear in love; but perfect love casts fear, because fear involves torment. But he who fears has not been made perfect in love.

B. **God Is With You on Your Journey**

- God constantly tells us in scriptures not to be fearful because I am with you.
- One of the most well-known scriptures, The 23rd Psalms, certainly confirms that God is with you. **Psalm 23: 4** says "Yea though I walk through the shadow of death, I will fear no evil; for You are with me; Your rod and Your staff, they comfort me. Most parents teach this scripture to their children at a very young age, and rightfully so.

C. **When You Look For God in Every Situation You Will Find Him**

- I encourage you to continue seeking God in your everyday activities. He will reveal glorious things to you that you never expected before. I pray that my story inspires you to "walk by faith and not by sight" (**2 Corinthians 5:7**).

- Knowing that your Heavenly Father is with you in unpredictable encounters, gives you *faith fuel* to press forward on your journey.

D. **Faith Fuel to Have God-Fidence like Abraham**
- **Genesis 12:1-3**, was written to show you and me as an example of blessings that come by obeying God and walking by faith, even in the most seemingly impossible situations.

E. **God Blessings Us Even When We Don't Deserve It**
- Abram did not exhibit God-Fidence in an unexpected stop in Egypt. He feared for his life and told Sarai to lie and tell Pharaoh that she was his sister. Even though Abram failed this test, God covered him with His protection, mercy and grace. Pharaoh recognized that God had His hand of protection on Abram and Sarai.

He blessed them with riches as they continued on their journey. The same is true for us when have failed to exude God-Fidence and walk in our God-given authority, God blesses us even when we don't deserve it.

F. Be Sure To Enjoy the Scenery on Your Journey

- On your road trip in life, be sure to enjoy the scenery along the way. Depending on where you are traveling from, you may see oceans, mountains, and even deserts. Either way, God will use every part of your trip for His glory. Not one stop or turn will be in vain. **Romans 8:28**, "And we know that all things work together for good to those love God, to those who are called according to His purpose."

G. God Created the Earth for You to Enjoy On Your Journey

- He intentionally created the earth as the only planet that humans could live on. The first book (Genesis) and first chapter of the Bible, clearly shows us that our Creator intentionally created an atmosphere for us to live and enjoy.

H. God's Plan for You Is Very Important to Him

- There are many scriptures that illustrate that God's plan for you is very important to Him. **Philippians 1:6**, "Being confident of this very thing, that He who began a good work in you will complete it until the day of Jesus Christ.

I. Your Life's Journey Has a Purpose

- God set you apart because of the purpose He has for your life. God won't change His mind so, you may as well embrace that fact.

J. **God Wants You to Have Balance on Your Journey**

- When you think of a journey, sometimes you may have the impression that is going to be tedious and unenjoyable. While this may be true, you will have difficult times as you are pursuing your life purpose; God also wants you to have pleasurable times. That is why we have holidays like Thanksgiving, Christmas and Labor Day. Marriages, births and graduations were also created by God to bring enjoyment to your life. **Ecclesiastes 9:7**, "Go eat your bread with joy, and drink your wine with a merry heart (but don't get drunk), for God has already approved what you do."

K. God Uses Every One of your Journey Experiences to prepare you for achieving your Goals

- Like going to school, every class you take, such as Math prepares you for more advanced subjects like Calculus and Geometry. God uses this same method to prepare you for more difficult stops on your life journey. Each mile of your journey can be likened to stepping up a ladder. Each step you take, positions you higher and higher. When you get to the top of the ladder, you are able to see things you could not see when you were on a lower rung. Below is scripture that confirms that God uses every juncture in your life to mature you for the future:

- **Hebrews 5:12- 14**, (12)"For though by this time you ought to be teachers, you need someone to teach you again the first principles of the oracles of God; and you have come to need milk and not solid food. (13) For everyone who partakes of only milk is unskilled in the Word of righteousness, for he is a babe. (14) But solid food belongs to those who are of full age; that is those who by reason of use have their senses exercised to discern both good and evil."

CHAPTER FOUR

The Power in Speaking Faith-Filled Words

On your journey, there will be times you will be tempted to speak words of defeat. No matter how hard it gets, don't do it! "Death and life are in the power of the tongue" (**Proverbs 18:21**). This chapter is probably the most important of all the chapters in my book combined. I cannot stress it enough that you have to adopt an unyielding determination to speak only faith-filled words about your life. That includes your marriage, relationship with your children, your health and finances. You must also reject negative words spoken over you, even if the person is joking. Words are powerful whether they are spoken by you or by someone else.

James, the brother of Jesus, describes the tongue as a small yet most powerful member of the body. He compares it to controlling the direction you want a horse to turn and a rudder that can steer a ship. He says a tongue has the power to set fires and can defile the whole body.

James, made more thought-provoking observations about the words we are capable of speaking, as shown in **James 3:2-12**.

- Men can tame animals but no man can tame the tongue
- The tongue when used for evil, is full of deadly poison
- Out of the same mouth, we can speak forth blessings and curses

James is emphatic that no man or woman should allow themselves to speak words that tear others down but use words that will build them up. When I think about James, I think about the fact that he grew up in the same household as his brother Jesus. If anyone has divine insight on the power of our words, it would be James.

Even though you cannot see words that are spoken, God can. He says He watches over His Word to perform it (**Jeremiah 1:12**). I am sure you have seen comic books or cartoons that show words in a caption. If you or others around you could see the words you speak, you would definitely be more careful about the words you let out of your mouth. Your words are packed with power.

I watched an interview of a well-known actor. He explained how when he has a strong desire to accomplish a certain goal, including getting a role for a movie, he speaks to it. He declares that it belongs to him. You and I have that same God-given ability. He went on to say that those who have made the most impact in the world, were gifted orators. Martin Luther King's most famous words, "I Have a Dream" and President John F. Kennedy's "It is not what your country can do for you, but what you can do for your Country" are just as powerful today as when they spoke them more than fifty years ago!

You Have the God-given Authority to Change Your Circumstances with Your Words

God made us in His own image (**Genesis 1:26**). This means we have the same attributes He has; particularly the ability to speak what we want. That does not mean we can speak things into existence that violate God's universal laws. We can declare His Word over our lives that aligns with His perfect will. About twenty five years ago, my former pastor's wife always quoted a phrase that I remember to this day. "Say what you want, not what you have, unless what you have is already what you want." That is a profound and true statement.

In **Mark 11:23**, Jesus tells His disciples, "For assuredly, I say to you, whoever says to this mountain, be removed and be cast into the sea, and does not doubt in his heart, but believes that those things he says will be done, he will have whatsoever he says. This scripture gives us insight on how potent our words and prayers can be. That is why we must be careful about what we speak. Speak that you are healed not that you are sick. Declare all your needs are met rather than you are broke. Quote scriptures that affirm that you are more than a conqueror, not man's words of defeat. Recite scriptures that build your confidence. Avoid reading random messages found in fortune cookies and news articles based on astrology. Only the truth from the Word of God should be trusted. In **Isaiah 55:11**, the Lord said, "So shall My Word be that goes forth from My mouth; it shall not return to Me void. But it shall prosper in the thing for which I sent it."

God framed the worlds with His Words out of literally nothing, by *faith* (**Hebrews 11:3**). You and I have the ability to frame the world we live in, by *faith*. Although we can declare our desires to materialize, we don't have the ability to create something out of nothing the way God can. With this understanding, it is crucial that we speak words that produce an environment we will enjoy.

We are not to use our words for deceitful outcomes. The world's system is already run by leaders that lie to gain more power or to cheat less fortunate citizens out of their inheritance. In **Genesis 3:1**, the serpent used shrewd words to get Eve to question what God commanded Adam. He twisted God's instructions, saying "Did not God say you could eat of every tree in the Garden." Eve answered him saying, "God said they could eat of every tree in the Garden except the tree in the midst of the Garden- the Tree of the Knowledge of Good and Evil. If she and Adam ate of it, they would surely die." Here is where the serpent told his big lie. He told her that they would not surely die and that God knew if they ate the fruit, their eyes would be opened, they would know good and evil and be like God.

By lying and twisting God's Words, Adam and Eve were kicked out of the Garden of Eden and sin entered the world. That was the beginning of the journey for you, me, and our families. This story shows that words can impact us and our families for generations.

What's In a Name?

To show you how powerful your words are, God brought all the animals on the earth to Adam to see what he would name them (**Genesis 2:19**). During Biblical days, parents named their children because of a certain situation, place or thing. This knowledge should definitely cause you to be careful about what you name your children. Depending on the name given to your son or daughter could set them on a journey of ease or difficulty. As an example, before the father of the twelve tribes of Israel's name was changed to Israel (meaning he wrestled with God and prevailed), his birth name was Jacob, which means trickster. Before God changed him, he lived according to the meaning of his name. He tricked his brother Esau out of his birthright (**Genesis 27:1-33**). Ironically, he was later tricked by his uncle Laban.

Laban misled Jacob by telling him he would give him his daughter, Rachel to marry after he worked for him without pay for seven years. After fulfilling his commitment, Jacob was fooled by Laban into marrying Leah, the unattractive older sister. When Jacob confronted his uncle about deceiving him, Laban's response was that their custom was that the oldest daughter had to be given in marriage before the younger daughter. He then told Jacob he would give him Rachel if he worked for him another seven years. Not only did Jacob serve Laban seven more years, he served him another seven years after he married Rachel. So Jacob ended up being tricked into serving Laban twenty-one years (**Genesis 29:1-30**)!

You and I can thank the Lord that God changed Jacob's name to Israel. Our Lord and Savior Jesus Christ came from the lineage of the twelve tribes of Children of Israel. God spoke a promise over His chosen people that cannot be taken back. That same promise is for all of us who have confessed Jesus as our Lord and Savior. The name Jesus is the name of above every name. His name in Hebrew, Yeshua means to save, to save alive, or to rescue. Knowing this, should give you more confidence, *faith fuel,* during your journey.

There is Power in the Name of Jesus

The name of Jesus is so powerful that the Lord God instructs us to pray to Him in the name of Jesus. In **John 14:13-14**, Jesus tells the disciples, "And whatsoever you ask in My name, that I will do, that the Father will be glorified in the Son. (Verse 14) "If you ask anything in My name, I will do it." On your journey you will have many situations where you will need to pray. In John 16:23-24, Jesus instructs His disciples to pray to the Heavenly Father in His name. And everything they asked the Father in His name, He would give it to them.

On a family cross country trip we visited the Grand Canyon. After leaving, we encountered a huge thunder storm. We saw tornadoes on each side of the highway. My son, Jy cried out, "Dad get us out of here!" It began to rain so hard, the highest speed of my wind shield wipers was not fast enough to see clearly.

I did not tell my wife and children that I was scared too but I was, lol! As I drove through the storm, I began to pray in Jesus' name to protect us and get us safely to our destination. I eventually found a rest area and parked until the rain stopped. A few hours later, we checked into a hotel and had a good breakfast the next morning. Like my son and I, there are times in life, when you will be afraid and will need to call on the name of Jesus to get to a safe place. It is comforting to know that we can pray in the name of Jesus, who is also our rescuer!

In the Old Testament, there are scriptures that prophesy of the coming of our Lord and Savior. He is also described in several majestic names. **Isaiah 7:14,** "Therefore the Lord Himself will give you a sign: Behold, the virgin shall conceive and bear a Son, and shall call His name Immanuel, God with us." **Isaiah 9:6**, "For unto us a Child is born. Unto us a Son is given. And the government will be upon His shoulder. And His name will be called Wonderful, Counselor, Mighty God, Everlasting Father, and Prince of Peace."

No matter whether you are meeting someone for the first time, going on a job interview or applying for a loan, the first question you must answer is "What is your name." It is not good enough to just give your first name. Your sir or last name identifies you. Imagine trying to cash your payroll check with just your first name. The banker would tell you to come back when your full name is on check. In every State, the law requires you to have a driver's license with your first and last name. If you are driving across the country and were stopped by the highway patrol, the first thing the officer will ask for is your driver's license. That officer is trained to run a check of your name and driver's license number to validate you have a legal right to drive.

Your family name means a lot. When King David showed he had courage to defeat Goliath, people wanted to know who his father was. It can open doors for you and unfortunately it can close doors for you. That is why it is imperative to have a good name (**Proverbs 22:1**). Your name not only travels with you but with your children and descendants as well. I have learned over the years to work diligently on having a good name. It makes your journey a lot smoother.

I AM That I AM

When commissioned Moses to free the Children of Israel from bondage by the Egyptians, he asked God who should I say that sent me? The Lord responded saying, tell them I AM That I AM (**Exodus 3:7-8**). This name conveys the Creator's dominion over all things, the source of power and His eternal nature. I AM. He is the self-sufficient, self-sustaining God who was, who is and who will be. When you get the revelation that everything you need comes from the great I AM, it makes your journey so much better. Moses went on to tell Pharaoh "Let my people go, as God had instructed him (**Exodus 5:1**).

The Seven Redemptive Names of Jehovah God

1. Jehovah-Rapha means *The Lord our Healer* (**Exodus 15:26, Isaiah 1:5-6, Jeremiah 17:9 and Luke 5:31**). It is a blessing to know that you can pray to God as your Healer for *faith fuel* along your journey.

2. Jehovah-Nissi means *The Lord our Banner or Refuge* (**Exodus 17:8-15, Psalm 20:5**). I don't know about you, but I am sure glad I can call on God for a safe hiding place in Him while I am on my journey.

3. Jehovah-Shammah means *The Lord Who is Present* (**Ezekiel 48:35, Exodus 33:14-15, 1 Chronicles 16:27, Psalm 16:11 and 97:5**). In other words, God is there whenever you need Him.

4. Jehovah Tsidkenu means *The Lord our Righteousness* (**Jeremiah 23:5-6, Psalm 11:7, 89:14 and I Corinthians 1:30**). It should be comforting to know that your righteousness is in God the Father and His Son Jesus Christ. Along your journey, there will have times you'll have to depend on His righteousness and not your own.

5. Jehovah-Shalom means *The Lord our Peace* (**Judges 6:24, Isaiah 9:6, and Luke 1:78-79**). There is nothing better than having peace on your life's journey.

6. Jehovah-Jireh means *The Lord our Provider* (Genesis 22:8-14, John 1:29, Galatians 3:8 and 1 Corinthians 2:7). Calling on God as your Provider should strengthen your faith. You will definitely need Him to provide for your needs along your journey.

7. Jehovah Ra'ah means *The Lord our Shepherd* (**Genesis 48:15, Psalm 23:1, 80:1, Isaiah 40:10-11 and 1 Peter 2:25**). Knowing God as your Shepherd should cause you to have faith that He is leading and guiding you along your journey.

I hope after learning more about the various names our Creator gave Himself lets you know how much He loves you and always planned for you to get to your desired place in life. Your confidence in God is like filling your heart with the highest and most powerful octane available. Praying to the Lord in His specific names for your specific needs is one of the keys to unlocking *Faith Fuel* for Your Journey.

Review of Chapter Four

Let's review some highlights from Chapter 4.

A. **The Power in Speaking Faith-Filled Words**

- On your journey, there will be times you will be tempted to speak words of defeat. No matter how hard it gets, don't do it! "Death and life are in the power of the tongue" (**Proverbs 18:21**).

- You must reject negative words spoken over you, even if the person is joking. Words are powerful whether they are spoken by you or by someone else.

- James, the brother of Jesus, describes the tongue as a small yet most powerful member of the body. He compares it to controlling the direction you want a horse to turn and a rudder that can steer a ship.

He says the tongue can set fires and can defile the whole body. James, made more thought provoking observations about the words we are capable of speaking, as shown in **James 3:2-12**. Men can tame animals but no man can tame the tongue. The tongue when used for evil, is full of deadly poison

Out of the same mouth, we can speak forth blessings and curses.

B. **You Have the God-given Authority to Change Your Circumstances with Your Words**

- God made us in His own image (**Genesis 1:26**). This means we have the same attributes as God, particularly the ability to speak what we want. That does not mean we can speak things into existence that violate God's principle laws but we can declare His Word over our lives that aligns with His perfect will.

C. **What's In a Name?**

- To show you how powerful your words are, God brought all the animals on the Earth to Adam to see what he would name them (**Genesis 2:19**). During Biblical days, parents named their children because of a certain situation, place or thing. This knowledge should definitely cause you to be careful about what you name your children.

D. **There is Power in the Name of Jesus**

- The name of Jesus is so powerful that the Lord God instructs us to pray to Him in the name of Jesus. In **John 14:13-14**, Jesus tells the disciples, "And whatsoever you ask in My name, that I will do, that the Father will be glorified in the Son. (Verse 14) "If you ask anything in My name, I will do it."

E. **I AM That I AM**

- When commissioned Moses to free the Children of Israel from bondage by the Egyptians, he asked God who should I say that sent me? The Lord responded saying, tell them I AM That I AM (**Exodus 3:7-8**). This name conveys the Creator's dominion over all things, the source of power and His eternal nature. I AM. He is the self-sufficient, self-sustaining God who was, who is and who will be. When you get the revelation that everything you need comes from the great I AM, it makes your journey so much better. Moses went on to tell Pharaoh "Let my people go, as God had instructed him (**Exodus 5:1**).

CHAPTER FIVE

The Power of Faith-Filled Prayers

Along your journey, you will run into situations where you need to pray. There will be a variety of things, including finances, health, marriage, children, parents, work and schooling will need to be presented to the Lord. The first thing you should know is, the Lord wants you to have confidence in your prayers to Him. **Philippians 4:6** says "Be anxious for nothing, but in everything, by prayer, supplication, and petitions with thanksgiving, let your requests be made known to God." Notice the phrases, "be anxious for nothing" and "with thanksgiving". Both imply that God answers prayers before you even get up off your knees. This is truly a blessing!

It is obvious that God wants you to have the assuredness that He will answer your prayers. That is why you can pray in faith. Praying in faith yields the best results. Often, how God answers your prayers will look different from what you expected. I remember late one evening, my car stalled in a remote area off the 71 freeway in Corona, California.

Unfortunately, at that time, I did not have roadside service. I tried calling a friend to pick me up. Not only did he not answer, his voice mail was full. I then called another friend who was unable help me. To make matters worse, two police cars showed up asking me questions and told me that I needed to move my car. Imagine that! Suddenly a stranger pulls up and offers to call AAA Roadside Service and charged the expense on his own account. This was *faith fuel* in action! I was able to get my car towed to a safe location. Being stranded on that dark road made me appreciate the power of praying in faith. I don't remember the details of how I got the car fixed but God made a way out of what seemed to be no way.

Praying the Word of God

When you pray God's Word over your circumstances, it activates His promises. As I shared earlier, God watches over His Word to perform it (**Jeremiah 1:12**). When you pray the Word of God as opposed to random prayers, your faith is strengthened. Here are scriptural prayers to pray for various situations:

1. Prayer of Protection- **Psalm 91: 1-16**
2. Prayer for Healing- **Isaiah 53:4-5, I Peter 2:24**
3. Prayer for Provision- **1 Chronicles 4:9-10**
4. Prayer for Peace- **Philippians 4:7, Psalm 23:1-6**
5. Prayer for Forgiveness- **1 John 1:9**
6. Prayer for Salvation- **Romans 10:9-10**
7. Prayer of Agreement- **Matthew 18:19**
8. Prayer for Victory in Spiritual Warfare- **Isaiah 54:17**
9. Prayer for Favor- **Psalm 90:17**
10. Prayer for Wisdom- **Proverbs 4:7**
11. Prayer for Confidence- **Hebrews 13:5-6**
12. Prayer for Direction- **Jeremiah 29:11**
13. Prayer for Guidance- **Matthew 6:31-34**
14. Prayer for Wisdom and Discernment- **1 Kings 3:9**

Praying in Your Heavenly Language

Every day presents a new adventure. Although you may have a daily routine, things can happen to interrupt your plans. You may have scheduled a business meeting or lunch with a friend. You may know the city where you want to purchase your dream home. As has happened recently, a shortage of available homes in the real estate market could throw your plans off. Your journey can be unpredictable.

Because of the Pandemic, many of us have had to cancel or delay our vacations. February 2020, my wife and I purchased airline tickets to visit our daughter, Driana and her family in New York. Because of my work schedule, we decided for her to fly to New York a week before me. During her visit the city experienced record breaking numbers of Covid cases. Reports of a lock down circulated. Soon, travelers would not be permitted to fly in or fly out of the city. Sondria and I got a check in our spirit for me to postpone my trip there and that it was best for her to cut her visit short.

Driana agreed with our decision. Had we neglected to follow the prompting of the Holy Spirit, our trip could have been disastrous. I am confident, praying in our Heavenly language made the difference.

There will be numerous times on your journey where you will have to make decisions that point in a different direction you were previously going. Praying in your Heavenly language or praying in the Spirit will give you the confidence you need to make the right choices. **Romans 8:26** "Likewise, the Spirit helps in our weaknesses. For we do not know what to pray for as we ought, but the Spirit Himself makes intercession for us with groanings which cannot be uttered." I love the phrase, and you should too, "the Spirit Himself makes intercession for us." That means you and I cannot mess up our prayers. Sometimes, we may have fear or condemnation in our heart that could hinder our prayers.

It is good news to know that praying in the Spirit guarantees that our prayers will reach God's ears, without it being tainted by our own issues.

Let's look at other scriptures that show the benefits of praying in the Spirit:

- **Jude 20**- "But you, beloved, building yourselves up on your most holy faith, praying in the Holy Spirit". This is again good news! At various intersections of your life's journey, you will need to be built up in your faith. Praying in the Spirit is like going to the gym and working out. It makes you stronger in the areas where you need strength the most.

- **Acts 2**:4 "And they were all filled with the Holy Spirit and began to speak with other tongues as the Spirit gave them utterance". On the "Day of Pentecost", the Holy Spirit visited the room where men of various languages came together to pray. They all heard the Spirit in their own language. This was the beginning of the Church as we know it.

Not long after that, 3,000 men and women got saved and became followers of Jesus Christ.

The Holy Spirit Gives You Power

There have been times on my journey when our lights were cut off or there was a blackout that caused us to lose power. If either of these events happened to you, I am sure you will agree that is not a good feeling. Imagine if you had to go through your whole life without power. You would constantly bump into things. You could break a toe or end up with a big hickey on your forehead, lol. You can't drive your car without battery power. When Jesus was about to ascend to Heaven, He promised the disciples that God would send them the Holy Spirit to give them power to live their lives in a way that would glorify God. In **Acts 1:8**, Jesus told them, "But shall receive power when the Holy Spirit comes upon you; and you shall be witnesses to Me in Jerusalem, and in all Judea and Samaria, and to the end of the earth.

Genesis 1:1-3 provides a vivid understanding of how powerful the Holy Spirit is: "In the beginning God created the heavens and the earth. (Verse 2) "The earth was without form and void darkness was on the face deep. And the Spirit of God was hovering over the waters. (Verse 3) "Then God said, let there be light; and there was light."

Luke wrote about these same instructions that Jesus gave to the disciples. **Luke 24:49**, "Behold, I send the Promise of My Father upon you; but tarry (wait) in the city of Jerusalem until you are endued with power from on high". It is very obvious the Lord wants us to be empowered to fulfill our assignment during our journey.

The beautiful thing about receiving power through the Holy Spirit is, its effects spill over to your children and your descendants. **Isaiah 44:3** "For I will pour water on him who is thirsty. And floods on the dry ground. I will pour My Spirit on your descendants. And will bless your offspring." All you have to do is ask God to fill you with His Holy Spirit. **Luke 11:13**, "If you then, being evil (a human being), know how to give good gifts to your children, how much more will your Heavenly Father give the Holy Spirit to those who ask Him!"

The Holy Spirit is so important to God that He warns us that blaspheming the Holy Spirit is the only sin that is unforgivable (**Matt. 12:31-32**). God also warns us about grieving the Holy Spirit in **Ephesians 4:30**.

The Holy Spirit is part of the Godhead as shown in **1 John 5:6-8**, "This is He who came by water and blood-Jesus Christ; not only by water, but by water and blood. And it is the Spirit who bears witness, because the Spirit of truth. Verse 7, "For there are three who bear witness in Heaven: the Father, the Word and the Holy Spirit; and these three are one". Verse 8, "And there are three that bear witness on earth: the Spirit, the Water and the Blood; and these three agree as one".

The Holy Spirit is a Helper, **John 14:16** "And I will pray the Father, and He will give you another Helper, that He may abide with you forever."

The Holy Spirit is the Spirit of Truth, **John 14:17** "Even the Spirit of Truth, whom the world cannot receive, because it neither sees Him nor knows Him; but you know Him, because He dwells with you and in you. **John 16:13** reads, "However, when He, the Spirit of Truth, has come, He will guide you into all truth; for has come, He will guide you into all truth; for He will not speak on His own authority, but whatever He hears, He will speak; and He will tell you things to come.

The Holy Spirit will teach you all things **John14:26** "But the Helper, the Holy Spirit, whom the Father will send in My name, He will *teach* you all things, and bring to your remembrance all things that I said to you."

Review of Chapter Five

Let's review some highlights from Chapter 5.

A. The Power of Faith-Filled Prayers

- Along your journey, you will run into situations where you need to pray. There will be a variety of things, including finances, health, marriage, children, parents, work and schooling that you will need to present to the Lord. The first thing you should know is, the Lord wants you to have confidence in your prayers to Him. **Philippians 4:6** says "Be anxious for nothing, but in everything, by prayer, supplication, and petitions with thanksgiving, let your requests be made known to God." Notice the phrases, "be anxious for nothing" and "with thanksgiving," both implies that God answers your prayers before you even get off of your knees. This is truly a blessing!

B. You Have the God-given Authority to Change Your Circumstances with Your Words

- God made us in His own image (**Genesis 1:26**). This means we have the same attributes He has, particularly the ability to speak what we want. That does not mean we can speak things into existence that violate God's principle laws but we can declare His Word over our lives that aligns with His perfect will.

C. Praying the Word of God

- When you pray God's Word over your circumstances, it activates His promises. As I shared earlier, God watches over His Word to perform it (**Jeremiah 1:12**). Your faith is strengthened when you pray the Word of God as opposed to random prayers. You can refer back to Chapter 5 to review scriptural prayers you can pray in various situations

D. Praying in Your Heavenly Language

- There will be numerous times on your journey where you will have to make decisions that point you in a different direction to where you were previously going. Praying in your Heavenly language or praying in the Spirit will give you the confidence you need to make the right choices. **Romans 8:26** reads "Likewise, the Spirit helps in our weaknesses. For we do not know what to pray for as we ought, but the Spirit Himself makes intercession for us with groanings which cannot be uttered."

E. The Holy Spirit Gives You Power

- When Jesus was about to ascend to Heaven, He promised the disciples that God would send them the Holy Spirit to give them power to live their lives in a way that would glorify God. In **Acts 1:8**, Jesus told them, "But you shall receive power when the Holy Spirit comes upon you; and you shall be witnesses to Me in Jerusalem, and in all Judea and Samaria, and to the end of the earth."

CHAPTER SIX

Think on Positive Outcomes

On your journey you will have plenty of time to think. So it is imperative that you realize what you think about consistently will determine your course and the place where you arrive. There is a famous quote often said by the Negro College Fund, "A mind is a terrible thing to waste." That is a very true statement. The Bible says, "As a man thinks, so is he" (**Proverbs 23:7**).

Guarding your mind is an everyday battle. When I was in the Air Force, airmen were responsible for guard duty. We were required to stand at the entry to our dorm while the others slept. As a young man, I did not appreciate the value in that assignment. I once paid another guy to take over my guard duty because there were gnats all over the walls. They were constantly flying into my face and ears. Lol. That is the way the journey can be. The enemy persistently tries to frustrate you with words and thoughts that don't line up with what God says about you. He tries to rob you of your confidence or use situations to get you mad. All the while, his goal is to get you off your post of guarding your most valuable gift- your mind.

To be successful in your thinking, you must fight to maintain positive thoughts. You should understand that" the weapons of your warfare are not carnal, but mighty through God, bringing every thought into captivity that exalts itself against the knowledge of God into captivity to the obedience of Christ Jesus" (**2 Corinthians 4-5**).

Have you ever driven somewhere and forgot how you got there? These situations tend to happen when you are driving to a place you routinely go to, like your job or your place of residence. In these instances, you lapse into unconscious thinking. During your journey, intentional or conscious thinking is best in order for you to arrive at your destination safely. Apostle Paul instructs us to intentionally think of positive outcomes instead of worrying about them in **Philippians 4:8**. "Finally, brethren, whatever things are true, whatever things are noble, whatever things are just, whatever things are pure, whatever things are lovely, whatever things are of good report, if there be any virtue and if there is anything praiseworthy, meditate on these things."

Intentional thinking takes work. It is easy to drift into unconscious thoughts, which is what the enemy counts on you doing. Anyone who has accomplished anything of value in their lifetime, did it because of intentional thinking or critical thinking. In fact, most employers appreciate and promote employees who exhibit good critical thinking skills. A person who is good at thinking on their feet or making good decisions quickly is greatly sought after in the job market. More and more, employers are investing in their staff by having them take Soft Skills training in addition to hard skills training. Critical Thinking is one of the Soft Skills. Having great critical thinking skills is important for business owners. The rise or fall of an establishment depends on how well they are able to address the concerns of their customers. They demand the businesses to provide them with solutions to their problems in a timely manner. CEOs and other C-level executives are required by their board members to have great critical thinking skills. Even in professional sports, the length of time of a coach's job is dependent on how well they are able to make decisions that help their teams win. I encourage you to spend time intentionally thinking about how you will handle various situations that may happen on your journey.

Creative Thinking

Much like critical thinking, creative thinking will be very vital on your journey. There will be times when a strategy that has worked in the past will not work today. That is why we need to pray every day, including praying in the Spirit, studying and hearing the Word of God on a daily basis. Faith comes by hearing the Word of God repetitiously (**Romans 10:17**).

Jacob needed a creative way to gain wealth in order to repay his brother Esau for stealing his birthright. After wrestling with the Angel, he fell to his knees and vowed to the Lord, that if He blessed him, he would give a tenth of everything he earned. Later God appeared to Jacob in a vision and told him to make an agreement with his uncle Laban. The agreement was for Jacob to receive the spotted and stripped livestock, put their food in a trough painted with spots and stripes. As a result, there was an abundance of cattle and sheep birthed that belonged to Jacob. When it came time for Jacob to leave with his family, Laban tried to back out of the deal but God had given Jacob a creative solution so he and his family could leave Laban's rule in peace and with wealth.

As it turned out, Esau had forgiven Jacob and refused the wealth Jacob had accumulated (**Genesis 30:25-36**). Hopefully, Jacob's transformational story increased your faith and you know that you learned no matter how bad your journey becomes, God will always provide a creative idea to get you back on track to your destiny.

I watched the movie, Think and Grow Rich based on the best seller book written by Napoleon Hill. The film version illustrated short stories of inventors and innovators, including, Thomas Edison, Henry Ford, Elon Musk, Andrew Carnegie, Alexander Graham Bell and Mary McCleod Bethune. These historic individuals exercised their God-given right and ability to think creatively. As a result, they impacted the world. You too have the same God-given right and ability to think of something that will make this world a better place. Our Master Creator said "let us make man in our own image" (**Genesis 1:26**). He thought about the universe before He spoke it into existence.

Creative ideas usually start with a problem that originates in a person's life and consumes their mind until they are moved to take action to produce a solution. You can tell when you have a creative idea that can be valuable to someone else, when your thoughts continue to consume your mind. The daughter of former slaves, Mary McCleod Bethune's burning desire was to learn how to read. She was so consumed with learning to read she walked five miles to her elementary school every morning, arriving early before any of the other students. Mary's passion for education grew and followed her through boarding school and seminary. She eventually became a teacher then started boarding school and college, Bethune Cookman College. In 1929, she was the first woman, black or white to start her own college.

During those times in the midst of the Great Depression, this was no small feat. Mary went onto serve as an advisor to U.S. Presidents, Franklin Roosevelt and Harry S. Truman. As a Civil Rights advocate, Mary held the position Vice President of NAACP from 1940 until she passed in 1955.

Needless to say, with all of her accomplishments, Mrs. Bethune tapped into creative thinking many times throughout her journey. I encourage you to study and meditate on the Word of God to tap into creative thinking. You can also research and read stories about others who have used their creativity to accomplish great things. Doing this will add *Faith Fuel for your Journey*.

Trust your Own Instincts

I pay attention to how animals operate on their own instincts. Because God gave humans the right and ability to make our own choices, sometimes we don't utilize our own instincts. The quality of our journey is directly tied to the choices we make and how we act on our instincts. Many battles have been won or lost based on how well we marry our instincts with our choices. During your journey you will be faced with situations that will require you to use both your instincts and critical thinking skills to make right choices. Let's delve into what is an instinct?

The Oxford Dictionary defines *instinct* as "a natural quality that makes people and animals tend to behave in a particular way using the knowledge and abilities that they were born with rather than thought or training." Unlike animals, as humans we have the ability to weigh what gives us an advantage in any given situation. When you rely on the Holy Spirit, we are able to adapt or make changes to our usual routines in order to obtain victory. Nevertheless, don't underestimate the power of listening to your God-given instincts. Knowing when to speak or be quiet can lead to amazing opportunities. Sometimes it is best for you to wait before taking action, and other times it may be most beneficial to take action quickly. Often, you will not have a definite reason for why you choose one or the other. It depends on your gut feeling or having peace or lack of peace in your spirit.

My life journey has involved a series of career moves that I instinctively made that paid off when it was all said and done. In the late 90s, the Lord gave me a nudge in my spirit that my employer at the time was experiencing serious troubles.

I had a dream there were padlocks on the doors and the employees could not get into the building. I had no proof that this dream would come true. I simply followed my instincts and listened to the Holy Spirit, applied and was hired for another job. A couple of weeks later, I found out that my dream came true. Some of my former co-workers went to work and the doors were locked and were not allowed to enter the premises. Not long after my former employer closed the doors permanently. By the way, the new job paid much more.

Many actors have trusted their instincts and landed lucrative film contracts by trusting their own instincts. Actor Tom Hanks chose to forgo a salary and opted to receive a percentage of the box office proceeds from the hit movie, Forrest Gump, which grossed more than $683 million! Famous actor John Travolta turned down that leading role. Although he made millions in other movies, I would not be surprised if John regretted not trusting his instincts and wishes he had accepted the role in this movie blockbuster!

Many people have come to regret not trusting the voice of the Holy Spirit and their own instincts when choosing someone they planned to spend the rest of their life with. If you are still on your love journey be sure to watch for red flags. Don't ignore them. That is God's way of getting your attention so that you don't make a life-long commitment to someone He has not chosen for you. Pray and ask the Lord if the person you are attracted to is the one who will prove to be the one who will be the right fit for you. There will be numerous bumps in the road along your journey and the quality of your marriage will be in direct proportion to the level of agreement that you and your spouse will have. In addition to trusting God, trust your own intuition and you will make the right decision. I call these instances on your journey unscheduled appointments.

Although these chance meetings are not on your calendar they are on God's. I will delve into this topic and how they will provide you with *Faith Fuel for Your Journey* in the next chapter.

Review of Chapter Six

Let's review some highlights from Chapter 6.

A. Think on Positive Outcomes

- On your journey you will have plenty of time to think. It is imperative that you realize what you think about consistently will determine your course and the place where you arrive. There is a famous quote often said by the Negro College Fund, "A Mind is a terrible thing to waste." That is a very true statement. The Bible says, "As a man thinks, so is he" (**Proverbs 23:7**).

B. Creative Thinking

- Much like critical thinking, creative thinking will be very vital on your journey. There will be times when a strategy that worked in the past, will not work today.

That is why we need to pray every day, including praying in the Spirit, studying and hearing the Word of God on a daily basis. Faith comes by hearing the Word of God repetitiously (**Romans 10:17**).

C. Trust your Own Instincts

- Because God gave humans the right and ability make our own choices, sometimes we don't utilize our own instincts. The quality of our journey is directly tied to the choices we make and how well we act on our instincts. Many battles have been won or lost based on how well we marry our instincts with our choices. During your journey you will be faced with situations that will require you to use both your instincts and critical thinking skills to make right choices.

The Oxford Dictionary defines *instinct* as "a natural quality that makes people and animals tend to behave in a particular way using the knowledge and abilities that they were born with rather than thought or training". Unlike animals, as humans we have the ability to weigh what gives us an advantage in any given situation.

When you rely on the Holy Spirit, we are able to adapt or make changes to our usual routines in order to obtain victory.

- Nevertheless, don't underestimate the power of listening to your God-given instincts. Knowing when to speak or be quiet can lead to amazing opportunities. Sometimes it is best to wait before taking action and other times it will be most beneficial to take action quickly.

Often, you will not have a definite reason of why you choose one or the other. It depends on your gut feeling or having peace or lack of peace in your spirit.

CHAPTER SEVEN

Unscheduled Appointments

There are times when you are in such a hurry to get where you are going that you may pass up great opportunities that will make your journey more pleasurable, sustainable and impactful. If you are like me, I am sure you reflected on a great opportunity that you walked by because you were focused on your own agenda at the moment. It could have been investing in stock that skyrocketed or a real estate deal that you passed on that another investor made a fortune on. I can't tell how many times I regretted not following my spiritual antenna about a situation that could have helped me further along on my journey.

I thank God that I did not miss my *unscheduled appointment* with my wife! A former coworker talked me into meeting a friend of his on a blind date. I canceled a previously planned date and opted to go on the blind date. When I arrived at her house, my future wife was there. She was a friend of the young lady I was supposed to meet. Instead, I was attracted to Sondria so I pursued her and I approached her in a way that turned her off. She immediately told me "I am not that kind of girl!" Needless to say, nothing happened that night. Lol.

Despite her response, I manage to get her phone number. I called her a few days later. I still had not learned my lesson and did not have the common sense to change my approach. This time she told me "If you can't come at me the right way, don't bother calling me again." Whew, she totally put me in my place! That caused me to have a level of respect for her that I did not have for other women at that time. She made such an impact on me that I could not stop thinking about her. Let my story be a lesson to you young men and women. About three months later I called again but her phone number was disconnected. Unbeknownst to me, she moved out of her apartment and went to live with her Aunt Trudy.

I thank God for second chances. About a year later, I was walking in the hallway where I worked for the Department of Public Social Services. Low and behold, here comes Sondria. I said to myself, "I am not going to blow this chance to get to know her". I showed that I good manners like my mother taught me. These are the words that came out of my mouth, "Hello young lady, aren't you Sondria?"

She answered, "You remembered my name." "Most people mispronounce my name." Obviously, I behaved like a gentleman from then on. The rest is history. We recently celebrated our thirty ninth wedding anniversary, have three children and five grandchildren. Talk about unscheduled appointments. I have often wondered what my life would been like if God had not placed the two of us at the right place and at the right time. He obviously had us scheduled to meet on His calendar! We were on a collision course to our divine destiny.

You Are On a Collision Course with Your Divine Destiny

I am reminded of the story of how Moses encountered the burning bush in the third chapter of **Exodus**. Right before this destiny changing moment, Moses was tending to the flock of his father-in-law, Jethro, leading them to the back of the desert. As he came to the mountain of Horeb, the mountain of God, an Angel of the Lord appeared to Moses in the midst of a bush as a flame of fire. This got his attention because the flame did not consume the bush, which is unnatural.

Moses was obviously very curious as to why this bush would not burned up, so he took a closer look at the bush. When God saw that Moses was intrigued by the bush, He said "Moses, Moses."

Moses answered God, saying, "Here I am." Allow me to insert this helpful side note, when there is something burning in your heart that will not go away, this could be an indication that God is showing you the assignment He has given you for your life. This could mean you have collided with your divine destiny.

By showing up, it will change the trajectory in your life. More importantly, it can change the course of history in a profound way for so many others, including your children's children, like it did for the Children of Israel. By Moses showing up, God saw that he was the vessel He would use to answer the prayers of His enslaved people, to set them free. When prompted by God, showing up, not only provides *Fuel for Your Journey*, it also fills the faith tank for countless others, especially your descendants.

At this point in the book, you may be asking God, how will I know when I being drawn to my burning bush? That is a good question. First, let's explore what this burning bush represents.

- I believe that it represents assignment. Just like the flame did not consume the bush in the presence of Moses, your God-assignment will continue to burn in your heart as long as you live.

- Even if you don't feel qualified, remember Moses was a stutterer, God will provide the help needed, as He did for Moses with Aaron, to accomplish what He destined you to do. All the Lord needs you to do is *show up*!

- Your God-given assignment will always benefit of others, not yourself. According to **Exodus 3:7,** God tells Moses, "I have surely seen the oppression of My people who are in Egypt, and have heard their cry because of their taskmasters, for I know their sorrows. In **Verses 8-10**, the Lord expounds on His assignment for Moses, ultimately concluding with choosing Moses to be the man who would go to Pharaoh to set His people free from slavery".

- Your past sins will not cancel out your assignment. Even though Moses had previously killed a man, God used him to lead His people out of slavery, through the wilderness to the promised- land. What is so powerful about the plan and forethought of God is He recognized that when Moses murdered the Egyptian, in his heart he was doing the right thing by defending one of his own Hebrew brothers. He noticed the same heart condition of Saul of Tarsus who was intent on destroying Christians because of his Jewish religious beliefs.

The next question you may be asking yourself is how do I *show up* so God can use me? Using the example of filling your gas tank to get to your desired destination, on your road trip you are always looking for road signs that show you how many miles away to the next gas station. Well, having that same mindset for your journey in life will prepare you for stopping at the right place where to fill up with faith for your life assignment. Imagine if you started driving across the country without noticing where the next gas station is located. What if you were running low on gas and you did not look at your gas gauge? Eventually, you would end up on the side of the highway calling for road-side service. All the while, placing you and your family at risk for a potential dangerous situation. Your life is even more important. You need to be aware of the conditions of your life and that means recognizing when your faith level is running low.

Famous comedian, Steve Harvey told the story about a time when he almost quit going after his dream. In the middle of calling his Mom to let her know he was packing up, he received a message alert.

This message was from the booking agent from Showtime at The Apollo. All Steve needed to do was *show up* for the gig. Of course, life is full of hurdles to leap over. Steve did not have the money to fly to New York. As he was about to hang up the phone with defeat on his mind, Steve heard another beep. This message was from a club owner in Florida saying if Steve could *show up*, he had a gig that paid $135. Since Steve was already in Florida, he had enough gas to make it to the club. Steve was so funny, the club owner booked him for a second night. As a result of God showing up for Steve at the most important juncture of his journey he was able to pay for a plane ticket to New York. Steve would later become he the longest lasting host in the history of Showtime at The Apollo. Talk about how God *shows up* to *fuel your faith* when you need Him the most! Steve Harvey's career was launched into the stratosphere.

Showing Up

Ultimately, *showing up* for your God-given assignment involves intentionally looking for post signs from God and listening to His voice. He will direct you to where He needs you to be at any given time along the journey.

Sometimes His voice is revealed through our spouse. I hate to admit my previous financial challenges but I developed a bad habit of buying ten to twenty dollars of gas, until I eventually could afford to it fill up. I made several trips to the gas station, when I could have just filled up the tank like my wife often suggested but old bad habits are not easy to change. Praise God, I finally got it, lol. Now, when I go to the gas station, I buy a fill tank of gas.

I can't believe I am telling on myself but, until 2020 when I tested positive for Covid, I did not exercise enough. I would hit and miss, honestly mostly miss. In my previous office job, I ate more fast food than I should have. At God's urging, my wife would ask me "What did you have for lunch today?" I could not lie. So I sheepishly admitted I had eaten a cheeseburger, fries and a soda or some other unhealthy meal.

Little did I know that there was a time ahead that would require exercising consistently and eating healthy foods that would better prepare me for fighting off the Covid 19 Virus. It does not feel good. I humbly admit that I was ignoring the post signs. With all that, through God's grace, mercy and His Sovereign Will for my life, I am still living and breathing. I take better care of my temple and I am motivated more than ever to live my life with the intent of *showing up* so I can fulfill my assignment.

God has a plan to use you for His glory. He is leading you to the next place to get *faith fuel for your journey*. All you have to do is *show up* and He will take care of the rest.

At this point in time, Russia has attacked Ukraine, causing the cost of gas to rise to record prices, worldwide. Especially in the conditions of the world today, no one in their right mind would drive past a gas station that is giving out free gas. By just *showing up,* you would get a full tank of gas without spending any of your own money. My friend, God offers to fill your faith tank every day and does not charge a penny. I want to encourage that you just when you are about to run out of faith, He *shows up* to fill your spirit right on time.

This disturbance caused by Russia, impacts the price of gas for the airlines, which in turn threatens the increase in airfare. The cost of food has surged and to make matters worse, there is also a food shortage. People around the world need to *show up* and get their free fill of faith more than ever. No one knows how long these conditions will last. The Bible says there will be wars and rumors of wars, nations rising against each other and famines and earthquakes in various places (**Matthew 24:6-13**). Global newscasts show these activities on a daily basis. No one can deny we are living in perilous times. It is critical to pull over on a daily basis to get *faith fuel for your journey.*

On your road trip, you know you have to make pit stops to get refueled for the remainder of your trip. Look for the signs on the highway that signal how many miles ahead until the next gas station. In the spirit, it is the same way, you look for signs for when you are running low on faith. The good news is you don't have to wonder how far the next place is for your faith to be refilled. It is in your Bible. With today's technology, you have access to the Word of God to you on demand. You can boldly enter the throne of God's grace to obtain mercy and find grace to help in your time of need (**Hebrews 4:16**).

Review of Chapter Seven

Let's review some highlights from the final, Chapter 7.

A. **Unscheduled Appointments**

- There are times on your journey when you are in such a hurry to get where you are going that you may pass up great opportunities that will make your journey a lot more pleasurable, sustainable and impactful. Take it from me, these seemingly circumstantial moments could positively change the trajectory of your journey.

B. **You Are On a Collision Course with Your Divine Destiny**

- Moses encountered the burning bush in the third chapter of **Exodus**. Right before this destiny changing moment, Moses was tending to the flock of his father-in-law, Jethro, leading them to the back of the desert. As he came to the mountain of Horeb, the mountain of God, an Angel of the Lord appeared to Moses in the midst of a bush as a flame. This got his attention because the flame did not consume the bush, which was unnatural.

  Moses was obviously very curious as to why this bush would not burned up, so he took a closer look at the bush. When God saw that Moses was intrigued by the bush, He said "Moses, Moses." Moses answered God, saying "Here I am".

Allow me to insert this helpful side note, when there is something burning in your heart that will not go away, this could be an indication that God is showing you the assignment He has given you for your life. This could mean you have collided with your divine destiny.

C. **Showing Up**

- Ultimately, *showing up* for your God-given assignment involves intentionally looking for post signs from God and listening to His voice. He will direct where He needs you to be at any given time on your journey.

- God has a plan to use you for His glory. Let Him steer your destiny vehicle to the next place to get *faith fuel for your journey*. All you have to do is *show up* and He will take care of the rest.

CONCLUSION

God Loves You

When I began writing this God-inspired book, *Faith Fuel for Your Journey*, the world had just began the spread and effects of the Corona Virus, leading to millions of people dying around the world. The Pandemic produced something we had never seen before in the Twenty First Century. Toilet paper and other essential items disappeared from grocery store shelves all over America.

Almost daily, we see video footage of people demonstrating hatred and violence towards each other. There has never been a greater need to know that God loves you in our lifetime.

I hope that what I was inspired to write demonstrates that God loves you. He has given me a mandate that every time I get a chance to write or speak to His people, to make sure I let others know that He loves you.

According to **1 Corinthians 13:8-13**, "Love never fails. It will never run out on you. You may pull over to a gas station and find out they are out of gas. Love is even more important than hope, and faith. You don't to worry, God's perfect love, through His Son Jesus, will cast out fear (**1 John 4:18**). He will always be with you and *show up* ready to fill you up at every mile and intersection of your life. He loves you too much to let you run out of *Faith Fuel for Your Journey*.

I could not have imagined that God would entrust me to write words that would mean so much at this time in human history. I pray that through the Creator downloading His words into my thoughts and guiding my fingers, you are inspired to hold onto positive expectations-HOPE. Thank you for joining me on this road trip, *Faith Fuel for Your Journey*. This may sound like a cliché but God loves you and so do I. God bless you and your family!

www.ingramcontent.com/pod-product-compliance
Lightning Source LLC
La Vergne TN
LVHW051240080426
835513LV00016B/1681